More Testimonials for
TATTOOS ON MY SOUL

"Passion, drama, humor . . . a cast of characters colorful enough to light up a Christmas tree . . ."

RYAN PHILLIPPE
ACTOR AND PRODUCER

"Talk about the Streetwise Way! A great read."

MACK 10
ARTIST AND CEO, HOO-BANGIN' RECORDS

"Burrel just 'flips the script' every time. He can turn any negative into a positive . . ."

BARON DAVIS
NBA PLAYER, #5 GOLDEN STATE WARRIORS

"The photographs are jaw-dropping, ghetto-fabulous!"

ROHAN MARLEY
DESIGNER/OWNER, TUFF GONG CLOTHING

"There's real heart and hope in this story. We can each learn from it."

DARRIUS D. MAC ROGERS
ENTREPRENEUR

"Man, this guy is something else! He has an amazingly positive energy that just never turns off. He's larger than life. He's unique . . ."

COREY MAGGETTE
NBA PLAYER, #50 LA CLIPPERS

"*Tattoos on My Soul* achieves something that most biographies fail to deliver . . . an intimate 'one-on-one' sensation that is only possible by sitting side-by-side with the storyteller. Burrel tells his story as though you and he are at the kitchen table. If possible, savor this book in one sitting with a nice bottle of wine, then, like me, look forward to the sequel. There must surely be one."

JOHN W. LEE II
CHAIRMAN, READY-TO-LEARN PARTNERSHIP

BURREL

Lee Wilks III

TATTOOS
On My Soul

From the Ghetto to the Top of the World

A Sizzling Story of Grit, Glitz and Personal Growth

For information:
Burrel Streetwise Inc.
1110 N. Lakeshore Drive
Suite 24N
Chicago, IL 60611

ISBN 0-9768736-0-5

Library of Congress Control Number: 2005929136

Interior Design and Editorial Services: The Roberts Group
(www.editorialservice.com)

Clothes by Haj Designs (www.hajdesigns.com)

In Memory of

Marshawn
Reilly
Pierre
Wenny
Paul
King Boo
Willie Cage
Maago
Big John
Big Bob
Dree
Fluke
Charles

Love you all.

Contents

CONTENTS

CONTENTS

Foreword

" I'm not the man I was and I'm not yet
the man I'm going to be. "
—Burrel Lee Wilks III

No Sugarcoating

I'M NO SAINT. NEVER WAS, NEVER WILL BE. I did a lot of wrong before I did right. A man can't be judged by his mistakes though, but by what he puts back along the way. When my personal balance sheet is totaled, I guarantee the credit will far outweigh the debit.

Let's face it: I'm an *ex*-everything. An ex-syrup-sucking, coke-tooting, gun-toting, gang chief, wrapped in the skin of a passionate, ambitious black man. There's little I haven't seen, haven't done, or had done to me. My days as a gang chief, hustler, and crook may be far behind me, but history can't be denied. We are the sum of our experiences—the good, bad, ugly, sublime, and *absurd*.

I can't separate myself from what I did as a young man but neither am I going to trail my past behind me like dirty linen, or unwanted baggage. For years, the ghetto was my home, my classroom, my livelihood, and my proving ground. I'm molded from this clay and shaped by these streets.

I have tattoos on my soul.

And What a Journey!

Extracting myself from the stew of narcotics, violence, fast money, and cheap life that was my birthright was tough; the wisdom acquired along the way, hard-earned. While on the road, I battled demons, won victories, and made just about every mistake a guy could make. I took knocks that would have leveled many a man and killed some. I lost friends and fortunes, experienced pain and betrayal, and did something no father ever should. I buried my son.

But I wouldn't have missed this ride for *anything*.

Fearless, thirsty, and passionate, I threw myself into life with the force of a hurricane, gusting full-speed through every door. More than a few slammed in my face—breaking my nose but *never* my spirit—and as if by magic, a thousand times as many opened wide in front of me.

You see I've never accepted that there's a *designated* place for me in this world. I believed when I was just a scrap of a kid, and still believe today, that I can achieve *anything* I set my mind to. With acute self-awareness, dogged self-reliance, and relentless resourcefulness, our personal possibilities are endless.

In the ghetto, you scrabble in the moment because you know, tomorrow may never come. Everything is short-term, immediate, instant; life chillingly cheap. The generations of young men lost to the bullet, needle, or penitentiary borders on genocide. If he survives an early grave, a kid from the streets will all too likely find his way into a different kind of tomb, behind the walls of drug addiction or prison.

Look at me: *conditioned* to be a crook, catapulted out of the cradle into a world of *doing wrong*. As a ghetto-born, African American male, a gang-banger and cog in the narcotics apparatus, what were the odds I'd make into my thirties?

I should be dead by now. My friends are, my son is, I've come close, but I *refuse* to be a statistic.[1]

---

1. In *Freakonomics: A Rogue Economist Explores the Hidden Side of Everything* (William Morrow, 2005), authors Steven D. Levitt and Stephen J. Dubner study four years of operating records, sourced from a single Black Disciples cell in Chicago. They conclude that those gang members, consistently active across that period, faced a *one* in four chance of being killed.

No Overnight Transformation

Mine is a rare, celebratory story of *transformation*. But if you're looking for an overnight conversion, a phoenix rising from the ashes, then I'm *not* your guy. I wasn't a *bad* kid who one morning woke up a *good* man. Real life is far messier and more complicated than that.

There was no blinding epiphany for me, no sudden moment of stunning clarity. I wasn't a nice, neat science project with a beginning, middle, and conclusion, and I wasn't born again. Transforming Buddy Burrel into the man he is today took determination, commitment, faith, *tenacity,* and *time.* It took me years to get my *Streetwise MBA,* and I'm still studying.

From gangster to life coach and from foolish boy to wise man, my growth was progressive: *evolution* rather than *reconstitution.* The man I am today is the sum of hundreds, even millions, of choices made, as I forged my own, unique path through life.

I am Burrel Lee Wilks III, and I am a *Master of Being Alive.*

Acknowledgments

No man's story is his own. Lives are ocean swells, ebbing and flowing around those who populate our past and present, splashing, saturating and sometimes breaking against them. To respect the privacy of individuals inadvertently caught in the current of my tumultuous life, identities, dates, and some details have been changed.

In addition to my first born, I am a man blessed with two wonderful daughters, both of whom make me proud. With respect for their right to privacy, I don't dwell in this account of my life, on the relationship I have with my girls, or with their mothers. If it leaves questions unanswered, forgive me.

It is with gratitude, respect, and affection that I acknowledge just a few of the folks who've been part of my life. There are, of course, *many* more. You know whom you are, and that I appreciate you.

Thanks to: my mom, Dad, Jackie, Marcel, Tweety, beautiful Troy, Pam Price (a special lady who has done a *great* job), Micky, my *wonderful* daughters Brittany and Peacabo, and Dante, my blessing of a grandson, and his family. Thanks too to brother Bobby Simmons, Brandi and nephew Bakari, Aunt Judy and family, Grandma Jonnie, God, Messiah, Bishop, Kevin Rice, P. Dub, Pope, Bobby Evans, Gamm, Rene, New York, Idealist, Vernon Harrison, California Tone, Keke, Prince Akeem, Dusko, JoJo Capone, Maurice McNeal Tony A, Weasel, Hineath, Codeine, Suge Knight, Sam McKay, Dino, Nemer Ziyad, Black, DMAC, Ron Vegara, Marcos Portugal, Dr. Jerry Lanier, Ed Bohlke, Ed See, Stan Matusiak, Rico, Stephen Todd, Jack Berger, Henry Ruzyc, Bill Stamatis, Carlton Knight, Carl

Portillo, John Lee, Frank Ward and family, and especially Jimmy, a fine young man, with enough spirit and character for us all.

Matt Carmody, immense thanks to you for your hands-on assistance, and practical advice, and also to Haj Designs. Haj, you're going to slay 'em!

Heart-felt appreciation for my wife and co–author, Janet, without whom my thoughts would never have found paper. And a word on words: this book is a collaborative effort, intentionally written in a manner that I hope readers find accessible and enjoyable. Don't be diverted by the lack of vernacular. The story is authentic. A word or two may be borrowed, but believe me, the life is *all* mine.

Any factual errors, apparent misrepresentations, or inconsistencies are strictly my own. Blame poor memory and misspent youth!

The Dark Horse

I do this 4 rings, the life, the struggle.
I became who I am because my essence is hustle
My nest is of orange leaves
I rest—not slumber
3 days ahead of the race
gotta work that number

Gentrified, genocide
I've seen 'em both
I sweat 4 no one my shirt remains soaked.
From Cortez to Wabash from highsides' to low rides
I stashed in my dash
Back @ the Grove . . .

I am the son of
Hot sauce with mild love
Negating yet dictating of what the style does
I speak the "King's Language"
A father, a truant
An ol' skool playa, who I influence? . . .
Success.

Marcel a.k.a. Mr. Greenweedz, 2005

Prologue

The police swooped as we drove through the gates of the River Forest Cemetery on that day in October 2002. I had just buried my son Marshawn. It was a still, sadness-sodden day. My eyes were gritty with grief, my throat scratchy, and my thoughts as fragile as cobwebs.

I'd seen watchers on the grounds but hadn't associated their presence with mine. Godfather was in the passenger seat, and, in a split second, we were surrounded by police cars, hemmed in, and ordered out by a band of Chicago's finest, guns drawn, cuffs rattling, bellies and biceps bulging.

My life as a gangster lay, like shed skin, far behind me. I'd just put my son in the ground, so close I could almost touch him. Yet in that moment, I knew I would always be judged in the present, based on a life I'd lived in the past.

I decided there and then: my story would be told.

CHAPTER ONE

Son Of Burrel

1967–1973 (The First Six Years)

A Bull Is Born

DEBUTING ON MAY 6, 1967, I WAS THE SECOND CHILD BORN TO Burrel and Gloria Wilks of Sacramento Street, in Chicago's West Side. Delivered at home, I arrived on time and, from the moment I popped out, was by all accounts a wriggling, boisterous bundle. A little Taurus bull with a thick hide and thicker head, I propelled my way into the world with enthusiasm, and then, like a toy with a run-down battery, simply stopped.

For the next eighteen months, I sat quietly on the floor while the Wilks household swirled around me. Watching and listening intently, I seldom uttered a sound or shed a tear. I was such a quiet presence, in fact, that one day my mom lost me. She turned the house and the neighborhood *upside down*, almost hysterical with worry. I'd fallen between the bed and the wall, it transpired, and had lain there, without a peep, for well over six hours!

> " *He just never moved. He didn't crawl or anything. Then the day he finally decided to walk, he hit the ground running. He hasn't stopped since.* "
> —Gloria Wilks

My father, Burrel Lee Wilks II—BL to his wife, Butch to his friends, but *always* a respectful *Dad* or *Father* to us kids—moved to Chicago at the age of nineteen. The only son of Jonnie Taylor, he was raised by his grandparents on a small holding in Mississippi. The Wilkses were a large, extended family, and for years, members of the clan had joined the mass migration of blacks escaping the oppressive hardship of rural life, and heading to all points north and west. My father's branch of the family tree gravitated north to the metropolis of Chicago, where the weather was less hospitable but the economy promised to be far *warmer*.

My father was one of the few who stayed down South long after other relatives had moved away. Burrel Lee was left to carry the weight back on the homestead. Pushed relentlessly by his grandfather to work harder and better, he tended crops, drove the tractor, milked cows, looked after the livestock, and was responsible for mountains of other chores.

School didn't play much of a role in Burrel Lee's strenuous, early-rising, backbreaking kind of life. My father didn't attend classes much past the sixth grade. The farm was his classroom; hard work his education. For his first eighteen years, he earned his keep with sweat, calluses, and aching muscles.

But Burrel Lee had something inside that set him apart from his peers: vision and ambition. He demanded more from life than the lot of a small-scale Mississippi agriculturist could possibly provide. The frustration of unfulfilled aspirations slithered and twisted inside him like cold, slippery eels.

During the early sixties, the Civil Rights Movement was reaching a crescendo. In 1963, Dr. Martin Luther King Jr. had delivered his groundbreaking, history-making speech in Washington. That same year civil rights leader Medgar Evers and President John F. Kennedy were both assassinated.

The year of 1964 was momentous, too. A landmark time politically, Congress passed the Civil Rights Act, declaring that discrimination based on race was illegal. In a dramatic crime that fired up national media frenzy, three civil rights workers were murdered in Mississippi.[2]

It was against this political backdrop that Burrel Lee continued to labor. As he broke his back on the farm, the flaming heat of these epic events passed him over without singeing a hair. But though neither formally educated nor politically active, Burrel was, without doubt, *politically inclined*. He knew what was going on in the world, and he understood it was time to take his place in it.

One night, late in the summer of 1964, he packed light and together with his common-law wife Gloria, set off to join relatives in the city of Chicago. I'm sure it didn't cross his mind the day he left, that many years hence he'd find his way back home to that farm in Mississippi.

Sanitation Work

Burrel Senior's first job in Chicago lasted more than fifteen years and proved to be an effective front for his real ambitions: to build a high-volume, high-profit, business empire.

My father was a lowly sanitation worker, employed by the local authorities. He swept streets, cleared debris, and rode refuse carts. Day after day, he breathed in the stinking, filthy stench of other folks' rubbish. But while hanging onto the back of those municipal trucks, his hands wrapped tightly in their leather straps, he began building his multimillion dollar narcotics empire. Burrel Lee planned to be *the* West Side kingpin.

He started with weed-dealing, a dime pack here and another there. Soon the packs became eighths and the eighths ounces, which became pounds. Before long Burrel Senior was the neighborhood's principal supplier of grass and high-grade coke.

Arriving home after a hard day straddling the garbage truck or sweeping gutters, he'd jump straight into the shower and scrub himself almost pink. He'd obsessively steam, shower, scrub, and soak, literally *sloughing* the day off his body. But Dad scoured off more than the smell

---

2. Extraordinarily, a key perpetrator of this crime was only brought to justice in June 2005, when elderly former Ku Klux Klansman Edgar Ray Killen was sentenced to sixty years in prison for the killings, a crime notorious enough to inspire the 1988 movie *Mississippi Burning*.

and the debris of the day when he showered, he also stripped away the imagined stigma of his menial job. Without fail, Burrel Senior presented himself to the world as a *winner*. He may have been a garbage man by day but his job, as sure as hell, wasn't going to define him in any other way. After showering, he'd don one of his *sharp* tailored suits, wax his dreadlocks, and head off into the night, *all* about business.

Sometimes he didn't come home for two or three days at a stretch, but it wasn't until I was eight years old that I learned what my father got up to on these nights away from home. I knew he visited his dealers and his *spots*, where he got down to the grimy business of cutting and shaking drugs, but I suspected, too, that he spent time with other women. A reality starkly confirmed when I was introduced to his "other wife."

My dad eventually had a second family with Amy; a fact he didn't hide from me, although he was less forthcoming with the rest of our family. This was another of the ways in which my father singled me out for *special* treatment. I was flattered, of course. Who wouldn't be? But by treating me as an adult from the moment I could talk, Burrel Senior heaped enormous weight on these young shoulders.

Green Thumbs

My dad had thumbs of pure green! In between the daily grind of work and his nocturnal outings, BL would retire to our modest garden—his *true* passion. He'd weed, prune, mow, dig, and plant for hours. When done for the day, he'd sit back and admire his handiwork, maybe sip a cup of coffee and smoke a joint or two.

Leaning back in his garden chair watching the world flow by, he appeared to be a man without a care. Meanwhile, behind the scenes, he continued to pull strings, push buttons, and make the moves required to build and manage a large, profitable drug empire. Soon business was flourishing as robustly as his rose bushes.

My old man had the best game plan of any operator out there. Hardnosed and pragmatic, he was prepared to do whatever it took to win. Few earned his trust. He was ever alert, and leery of nearly everyone, so it was natural that his core team was comprised mostly of relatives, including his closest confidant, Charles. Raised under the same roof in Mississippi, Charles and my father were *partners in crime* from the get-go, an important relationship that would thrive for decades.

Before long, Burrel Senior had opened up supply channels to a major Mexican cartel through a local middleman, Tom. By now, he was receiving drugs—coke, marijuana, and soon heroin—literally by the *truckload*. He converted these into sacks of cash by pushing the merchandise through the prolific sales network he'd created.

The supplier-seller relationship was sound enough for Tom to agree to take payment on the back-end, after Dad had taken off his *gapper.* Some nights the volume of the delivery was such that it took the best part of an hour to unload the goods. Our homes on Sacramento Street, and eventually Cortez, would be packed to the brim with mountains of bricked and compressed marijuana, parceled in Saran Wrap. The heady smell of weed permeated every corner of the house and was more familiar to us than eggs and grits.

My father's crew was strategically positioned to leverage a number of secure distribution channels. One cousin supplied local government workers, while Charles filled the demand generated by the workforce, two thousand strong, at the local Ford plant where he worked.

The money rolled in as predictably as the tide. My job was to count it, and count it I did, until my fingers bled from dozens of little paper cuts. I handled $1 million or more in a week. When income outstripped spending, Burrel Senior had a simple solution: he planted the stuff in the garden!

Getting up in the small hours, he'd head downstairs and out into the night air. He'd then bury mounds of bills, bundled in black bin liners, in shallow pits under the lawn. Initially, the notes were Saran Wrapped, but the packaging had to become more sophisticated after dampness seeped under the plastic a few of times, turning the notes soggy and blue-green with wet ink and mold. After that, Dad custom-designed some steel containers for the job.

So there was my father: sweeping the streets, emptying bins, and riding the back of a garbage truck by day, while by night, like a graverobber in reverse, clandestinely burying huge caches of *scratch* in the garden.

My Icon

Burrel Senior, a naturally imposing figure and a born leader, was a hand-some man. Light-skinned, slight but sinewy, he had long, Jamaican-style dreadlocks and an infectious white smile. At 5'9" he wasn't physically large, yet he was one of the most impressive men you were ever likely to meet. He wielded this air of natural authority with the force of a baseball bat.

Charming, easy company when he wanted to be, he was a master at separating the *emotional* from the *financial*. Sentimentality rarely clouded his judgment, and his ability to make decisions objectively, without allowing friendship to get in the way, was *cold*. At other times, he would be all but consumed with a righteous and frightening fury. Countenance contorted with rage, he'd appear to lose all reason in the heat of the moment. It was just an illusion though. Ultimately, Dad was *all* about control.

I came to realize that his rages, his charm, and his icy implacability were simply alternative weapons in a well-stocked armory. Here was a man *totally* and *absolutely* focused on the business of doing business. A pure force of nature, my old man was wily, charming, and deeply manipulative.

I admired, feared, respected, and loved him. To me, he was the *hippest* guy in the world. He lived life as though he were starring in a movie. I thought everything he did was super-*smooth,* and more than anything else, I wanted to *be* him.

From the beginning, I was his miniature apprentice, but even as I emulated him, I quietly nurtured the idea that anything he did I could do just as well. At this tender age, I didn't recognize the first faint stirrings of rivalry. Over time, the tension between us would only grow, but for now, my father was my hero.

Burrel Senior kept a tight hold on the family purse strings. The profits rolled in, but housekeeping allowances were stingy. Us kids didn't go short of anything, but Dad liked to keep Mom on her toes. That's largely why she had to keep working as a secretary at the Illinois Masonic Hospital. Her job probably saved her sanity, too. The hospital provided respite. It was a place where she could "get out from under," spend time with friends, and avoid the fallout from BL's erratic, often violent moods.

The family I was born into was powerful and respected then. Materially we went short of little, my mother gave us all the emotional support she could muster, and my dad provided the discipline. We had access to a world most kids couldn't even imagine. As an irrepressibly ambitious kid, it was an intoxicating life. Literally.

When I was two years old, Burrel Senior would blow marijuana smoke in my face. At three, he'd take me with him, carrying me on his shoulders, as he went about business or attended to social calls. We were Big B and Little B. He appeared proud of his namesake.

Sitting by quietly, while he conducted business, I'd spend hours in smoky rooms inhaling those good, green fumes; eating up every word, expression, and nuance. I smoked my first *official* spliff at seven, courtesy of my dad, and after that, would regularly join the men as they puffed their way through a joint or two.

Mind Jedi

My father may have been infamous for his volatile temper and sometimes violent outbursts, but paradoxically, he also cultivated the art of quiet leadership. The complex choreography of human interaction fascinated me, and I studied diligently.

By scrutinizing group dynamics and body language, I learned to read a meeting's subtext. I watched and listened intently, staying awake into the small hours, eyes darting everywhere. During these long sessions, I honed my ability to read a person's character, and intentions, in a split second: a skill of the highest value in a world where misjudgment could result in a killing or incarceration.

Men smoked, gambled, argued, got high, and passed around wisdom and money. Tempers flared, tempers were doused, and my father conducted it all like a *maestro*.

In a group situation, he would usually assume an air of detachment. Leaning back in his chair, he'd quietly smoke and assess the activity. He radiated an aura of authority that was almost tangible. The other guys might argue, haggle, joke, and debate, but they *always* kept one eye on my father, carefully gauging his reaction. By the end of any session, my old man was usually holding court. Like iron filings to a magnet, Butch would bring the game to him.

By accompanying my dad on these occasions, I developed the greatest respect for *age* and *experience*. Sitting at his knee, I'd listen avidly to the older guys he kept company with. The insight accumulated by those men was like a gift if you only took the time to unwrap it. Like my father, some of his peers had come to Chicago from the South. Stories of segregation and injustice were etched deep on their faces, and the promise of opportunity and fortune filled their heads and words. I look back with awe at the character, strength, and stoicism of some of these men who'd struggled through hardships beyond the imagination of most of us today.

Politics and Power

My old man intuitively understood the *politics* of power, and the *power* of politics. He had an impressive grasp, more sophisticated than one might expect of a Mississippi farm boy, of just how to manipulate both. Burrel Senior understood about connections. He knew it was *who* you knew even more than *what* you knew. A few debts in the favor-bank, he hoped, would smooth the way and provide him the elbowroom he required. He understood the age-old language of greased palms and scratched backs, or what we in our neck of the woods called *the Chicago way*.

The late sixties and early seventies were a time of turbulence for black inner city communities in Chicago. After a brief flirtation with respectability, street gang membership and inter-faction rivalry exploded. The larger gang organizations ruptured, splintered, and became virtually ungovernable. The streets, awash with narcotics from all corners of the world, were battle zones.

Drug use and crime rates soared upwards, and Mayor Daly's response was to declare "war on gangs." But even as the authorities clamped down, the streets were becoming all but impenetrable. Walking down our block was like walking into an urban minefield, guns and gold glinting on street corners, smoke and testosterone hanging in the air. The gulf between the *establishment* and inner city residents grew more yawning by the day.

It was logical, then, that local authorities looked to influential residents—men like Burrel Senior—to try and bridge that gap and become conduits to the community.

When we lived on Sacramento Street, my dad was chosen as the precinct captain. In this capacity, Burrel Senior worked closely with the local alderman; his job was to mobilize the community in support of the alderman's reelection. Pulling together teams of runners, he'd take on much of the campaign legwork: distributing flyers, posting posters, or just spreading the word throughout the neighborhood.

His badge gave him significant leverage with the local authorities, although as it turned out, not enough to cover our asses or shield him from the unwelcome attentions of the law. His connections did give him an edge though. After an ill-advised narcotics deal with a local informant, Burrel Lee was given a heads-up by the local police, that unless he made some quick adjustments to his lifestyle, he was in *big* trouble.

He decided, instead, to make himself scarce. It was time to move on.

CHAPTER TWO

Cortez Street

1973–1974 (Age 6–7 Years)

New Kids on the Block

WE ARRIVED ON CORTEZ STREET IN 1973 WHEN I'D JUST TURNED SIX.

In the heart of the West Side, Cortez was situated one block off Cicero, five blocks off Chicago, and four blocks off Division. It was a roughneck area, but a mere fifteen-minute drive east could transport you to the heart of the *old money* enclaves hugging the shores of magnificent Lake Michigan: Chicago's exclusive Gold Coast.

Before reaching the Gold Coast, however, you hit the infamous Cabrini Green Projects on Division, and by pointing your car south and driving a few miles, you'd come up against the Rockwell and Argyle Garden Projects. Termite nests of trouble, these developments were originally conceived as enlightened experiments in urban planning. By the seventies, when we moved to Cortez, they'd decayed into perfect little petri dishes of crime.

Their physical attributes—high-rise, anonymous, and run-down—made them easy to defend, and the gangs had long since headquartered themselves comfortably in these mini-fortresses. Riddled with elaborate escape routes, they were warrens of holes, tunnels, and walkways. Given their proximity to Cortez, violent overspill from these gangland hothouses was inevitable, and the sound of gunfire a common occurrence on our street.

Cortez and the surrounding settlements along Lamon, Cicero, Augusta, Walton, and Iowa were typical ghetto neighborhoods. Barbershops, social clubs, grocery and liquor stores, fast food outlets, and car repair shops were punctuated every few doorways or so, by one of the dozens of small places of worship that seem to spring up like weeds in areas of acute deprivation. The Centre of Hope, The New Way, The Three Crosses of Calvary, The Fellowship Church, Mount Carmel, The New Light Holiness Church: spiritual sustenance—and collection plates—apparently came in any shape and flavor you fancied.

Some days Cortez felt like a war zone, and we'd pick our way through it as cautiously as if walking on razor blades. On other days, the street adopted a much sunnier persona, and for a while, we'd feel like any small, connected community. Lined with unpretentious but solid houses, front stoops facing onto modest front yards, local folks would gather on fine days to exchange news and gossip. In any community, rumor and hearsay are highly valued currencies. The day we arrived the place was abuzz.

Siblings

By now, we were three kids. Theresa, usually called Jackie, was the eldest by two years. I was next in line. Marcel—born on Sacramento Street a couple of years before we moved to Cortez—was four years younger than me. My mom had her hands full when we relocated from Sacramento. I'd just turned six, Jackie was seven, and Marcel was toddling through his terrible twos.

Jackie was tremendously talented. The most naturally gifted of us all, she sang beautifully, but Dad had little patience with the idea of her forging a career in the music business. Jackie's singing reputation spread. During her teens, she was in great demand by some of the most popular local performers who wanted her to front them, but my dad put his foot down. He banned her from taking to the stage.

Marcel looked up to his big brother the way I looked up to my dad. Though protective toward him, that didn't stop me from goading and prodding him, whenever I could, to take part in whatever mischief I was up to, and buying his silence when coercion failed. I spent half my time running interference, deflecting the heat, and the other half planting his feet firmly in the fire!

My sister Rakisha—Tweety—arrived later. She was the baby of the family and was a full eight years younger than me. Her relationship with Dad reflected that age difference. She didn't bond with him the way us older kids did, and so was neither *lavished* nor *lashed* in the same way. She and I were two peas in a pod though—tenacious, driven, and determined. For a long while, we were the best of friends.

> *My brother was a trickster. He was always bribing me. Yeah, Burrel was the king of trickery. He'd always bribe me to be quiet with the promise of a 'Mr. Rogers trolley', you know, the one that used to take Mr. Rogers from his house to the Land of Make Believe. He promised me that trolley for years and years . . .*
> —Marcel Wilks

In some ways I guess Dad spoilt me, but he also set the bar high. From the start, his ambitions were conflicting. On one level, he wanted me to be a true reflection of him—his protégé, partner, and heir—but simultaneously, he needed to hold me in check. In reality, there was room for only *one* Burrel Lee Wilks at the top of our family tree. Dad guarded his power jealously. With one hand, he pulled me along with him, while with the other, he pushed me firmly back down.

I'm certain all father-son relationships are complex and fraught with apparent contradictions. Ours was no exception. I loved my father and appreciated everything he did for me, but he was one uncompromising *son of a bitch*. It wouldn't be long before we were butting horns.

Block Club President

On our arrival at Cortez Street, it was clear, from our reception, that Dad's reputation had preceded him. Folks were respectful and a little fearful. It seemed natural then, that after only a few months in residence,

Burrel Senior was chosen as block club president, a position with significant status attached.

The role of block club president was more neighborhood-oriented than that of precinct captain. The block club president organized and coordinated various events for local residents—parades, dances, cookouts, and parties—activities designed to build a sense of solidarity and community.

For my dad, being block club president meant more though. His position enabled him to open up communications with the local authorities, stay cool with the police, and win some influential friends. He used his position to grease the political wheels and smooth his way business-wise. The badge provided a welcome cloak of respectability. Burrel Senior knew how to work the system and, when necessary, how to hide within it.

Tough Love

Boss of the streets, my old man was a *despot* in the house. He was *ol' skool* and then some! An unyielding, unbending disciplinarian, we all danced to his tune. The Highway Code had fewer rules than we did at home. We couldn't play ball on the street, walk on the grass, have friends sit on the porch, eat too much cereal, or play tag. In fact, most of the activities in which a boisterous young boy loves to get tangled were forbidden under my dad's roof.

Dad's tyranny wasn't restricted to our household. He may have sported the badge of block club president, but in reality, this was nothing more than decorative. My father didn't *need* any badge of authority. At the end of the day, the only say-so he required and respected was his own. He viewed Cortez as his territory, appointed himself neighborhood watchdog, and didn't shy away from his duties.

No one messed with Burrel Lee Wilks II.

If some hapless stranger were spotted sitting on the grass a few houses away, minding his own business, my dad would be over there like a shot. The unfortunate guy would be abruptly rousted from his reverie and ordered off the property. If he weren't obsequious enough, Burrel Senior would pull out a gun and wave it in his face. That *always* achieved the desired effect.

The man with the X-ray eyes, perpetually scanning his fiefdom, never missed a thing at home either. In fact, he reserved his most penetrating scrutiny of all for those closest to him. Burrel Senior practiced some of the *toughest* tough-love imaginable.

The mood barometer in the Wilks' household was governed almost entirely by my father's frame of mind. Unlike the weather, his mood couldn't be predicted based on an analysis of "prevailing conditions," so we'd all tiptoe around until we figured out which way the wind was blowing that day. If for any reason he was in bad humor—which was often—we'd know it sooner rather than later.

Dad was using narcotics more heavily these days, and his daily diet of uppers and downers bequeathed him colossal, cranky hangovers. It took little to trigger an outburst. He was easy to anger and hard to placate. Any challenge to his authority—real or imagined—uncorked a reaction that put the fear of God into us all. Dad wrote all the rules and was uncompromising in their enforcement, by hand, boot, or belt!

I was thrashed—probably hundreds of times—right up until the time I left home. An irrepressibly naughty boy with the stubbornness of a bull and the thick head to match, I was *perpetually* in trouble, my infractions way too many to list. I'd dip into Dad's money, smoke his weed, track mud onto the carpet, break a cup, or empty the cereal packet. I'd be caught fighting, playing hooky, walking on the grass, stealing Marcel's birthday money—you name it, I was probably guilty. As a consequence of my relentless mischievousness, I faced the full force of Dad's fury more frequently than anyone else.

> My dad was totally inconsistent. Sometimes he'd just turn a blind eye, and other times he'd beat the shit out of you for nothing. I remember once he kicked the crap out of me for walking on the grass. I had welts on my back for weeks.
>
> —Marcel Wilks

Sometimes all but apoplectic with rage, he'd yell and scream, the veins on his neck standing out like cords. He'd whip me until I bled, using anything that came to hand. His favorite weapon, and my most loathed, was a thick leather dog leash knotted six or seven times. On one occasion—one I'll not forget in this lifetime—he thrashed me with a plastic-covered extension lead.

Coffee Grinding

One of the worst beatings I ever took from my dad came on a fateful day, in the summer of my sixth year.

Everything about him fascinated me. I'd be the first one up in the morning so as not to miss a moment of his *conversation* or a second of his *demonstration*. When he emerged from bed each day, often quite late, the first thing he'd do was to take a seat at the kitchen table and carefully roll a joint. I'd already be there, sitting in my underwear, eagerly awaiting my cue. Like clockwork, after taking a few puffs from a fat joint, Dad would get up and head outside to the garden. That's when I'd start preparing his cup of morning coffee.

I relished this ritual. A privilege of sorts, it allowed me to showcase my culinary skills—I made a *mean* cup of coffee—but it also gave me some precious, private moments with the old man. I loved sitting with him in the garden while he sucked up his first caffeine-fix of the day and slowly came to life.

This sense of privilege didn't get in the way of me taking a few short-cuts though. Putting the pan on the gas ring to boil the milk for Dad's coffee, I'd grab some toast for my own breakfast at the same time. There was nothing in the world to stop me from making *two* cups of coffee—one for him and one for me. But there was something special about my old man's coffee—milky, sweet, and, well, *his*.

So rather than make a second cup for myself, I'd fill his mug to the brim and soak up the surplus by dipping in my toast a few times, taking care to scoop out the crumbs. Then I'd take it downstairs, taking great pains not to spill a drop, to where he sat in the garden.

I got away with it for a long time—until the day I got lazy and left a scum of crumbs floating on the surface of his morning beverage. I denied all charges, of course (*not smart!*), and my father beat me to within an inch of my life. I've never touched coffee since.

Sure, I learned a tough lesson about the price of taking shortcuts, but mostly what I learned was that if you're going to lie, then at least be smart enough to *never, ever* get caught!

Cold Cuts

The punishments I dreaded the most were the ones served cold. I'd cross my dad on something, and though there would be no immediate reaction from him, I knew I hadn't gotten away with anything. He might not be in the mood to kick my ass right then and there, but that was okay—we both knew it would keep. His body language and demeanor made clear, this was *far* from over.

Simmering, sometimes for days on end, Dad would work himself up into a righteous funk. In the meantime, doom hung over my head like a guillotine on a hair-trigger. In hindsight, I think Burrel Senior may even have relished these *slow-burn* situations. With my fate firmly in his hands, he could take his time, play his mind games, and savor what was to come, rolling it around in his head like a different kind of high.

I look back at those times with mixed feelings. My punishments were harsh, yet I know I deserved much of what was meted out. I relentlessly tested this *ol' skool* disciplinarian, and he, in turn, taught me the most fundamental lessons of my young life. I've no doubt he loved me, but his *need* to rule me was stronger. Dad just had to be in control.

Counting Cash

Though regularly escorting my old man out and about as his protégé, I wrestled, too, with a formidable roster of chores at home. First and foremost was the vital task of counting the weekly take from his narcotics business.

To some, this might sound like a fantasy come true. Imagine, stacks and sacks of green dollar bills heaped up in loose piles, spilling and flowing over onto the floor. But if you've ever had to handle large amounts of cash, you'll know just how *filthy* this stuff really is! The cash I counted came straight from the streets, as dirty as it gets, and I had to bury myself, up to my elbows, in mounds of grimy, germy, sticky bills.

I shuffled paper until my hands were covered in tiny cuts and my fingers bled. While I was at it, I extracted my fee, a couple of thousand bucks straight off the top. I became so slick at counting *scratch* that on occasion my dad would accuse me of cutting corners. Claiming I hadn't done the job thoroughly, he'd kick the precarious piles over, and tell me to start again. Trembling with frustration, I'd get my own back by skimming off another couple of G's, telling my dad he was right, I had indeed miscounted the first time around.

Years later he admitted that he'd always known I was robbing him blind. By his logic though, anyone regularly counting millions of dollars was going to steal a few, and he'd prefer it be his son than some *"street-nigga* he'd have to hurt."

My other tasks included walking the dogs—like many families in our neighborhood, we bred pit bulls—cleaning the stairwells and basement, mowing lawns, mopping the floors, and vacuuming. Burrel Senior would hover around directing, dictating, and, if he was in the mood, kicking my butt. Sometimes he'd make me do a task over, just because he could.

One of the few diversions guaranteed to distract my old man was a good movie. He particularly loved *ol' gangsta* flicks, Kung Fu, and westerns. Anything featuring Bruce Lee, John Wayne, James Cagney, or Humphrey Bogart, guaranteed a few hours respite from Burrel's Law and Order.

He liked company when he watched a movie but would become so engrossed in the story that, after twenty minutes or so, he was oblivious to everything but the screen. As soon as I saw he'd gone into the "zone," I'd slip away unnoticed—until I got hooked on movies myself. After that, we'd sit side by side for hours on end, like a couple of zombies, hypnotized by those flickering images.

When chores stretched out in front of me, it just about killed me. I was a bundle of energy, always champing at the bit. It seemed that there were *a thousand* more important things that *I needed* to be doing. Perpetually in a rush, I cut corners whenever I could in order to get about my business, a high-risk strategy that resulted in many a painful thrashing!

Family Values

My mother, a hard-working, sweet lady, was subjected to considerable emotional and physical abuse at the hands of my dad. Although I came in for more than my fair share of thrashings, my punishments were often, in some way, provoked. Not so for Mom. She usually bore the brunt of Dad's temper for no discernible—and certainly no justifiable—reason.

My parents never married. In fact, Dad kept a number of casual mistresses, and had his second "secret" family. Amy eventually bore him two sons. It wasn't an uncommon situation in our neighborhood for a man to have more than one family, but my dad's behavior was hard on my mom. The betrayal was compounded by the fact that even his own blatant faithlessness didn't deter BL from sometimes accusing Gloria of cheating on *him*.

Beaten regularly by Dad for imagined wrongs, Mom was fearful and cowed. She walked on eggshells around him. Us kids were caught between the two of them. I hero-worshipped my father and nurtured a deep desire to emulate him. My love for my mom ran just as deep but wasn't tinged with the same levels of fear and idolization. My affection for her was softer and more difficult to define.

Mom, who was a secretary at the Illinois Masonic Hospital, worked hard. Every day she took the CTA Cicero bus to Addison, where she caught another bus to Belmont, a journey taking forty minutes or so each way. Come rain, shine, or Chicago snow, my mom made that trek. In more than twenty years, she never took a day's sick leave and was valued highly at the hospital.

So here we were, the somewhat dysfunctional family of a fabulously wealthy "drug-lord," yet each day our dad rode the back of a sanitation truck and our mom the bus, in order to labor eight hours a day, five days a week, for minimum wages. It was one of those incongruities we learned to live with.

On occasion, Mom would miss the bus home at the end of her shift. How she must have feared going home on those days. If the old man were around and in a mood, he'd shout, threaten, and, as often as not, land a few blows. It was hard for a young boy to watch the mother he loved being beaten. But my dad always told me to stay out of it. He said I couldn't comprehend the ways of adults. When I grew up, he explained, I'd appreciate why he did what he did and only then would I understand why my mother had deserved such treatment.

In my heart, I knew this was bogus. On one level, I recognized the double standards he practiced and preached and knew he treated my mom disgracefully. On another, I wanted to buy his explanation. I was just a kid. These were the only ways I knew, and Mom seemed to accept the hierarchy, the rules, and the abuse. I couldn't imagine things being different.

At eight years old, I told my mom when she was ready to stand up to the old man I'd stand with her, but I wouldn't stand alone.

CHAPTER THREE

Buddy Burrel

1974–1975 (Age 7–8 Years)

Sparrows

BY THE TIME I WAS SEVEN, THE ELDER BURREL HAD INTRODUCED ME TO MARIJUANA AND MADE ME A LIEUTENANT IN HIS SMALL ARMY. He had no intention of getting burned, ever again, by small-time informers the way he had on Sacramento Street. From now on, he intended to fly only with the *eagles*, not hop around with the *sparrows*.

This suited me just fine. I'd always believed I could do anything my dad could. I enjoyed the kudos of being the *Son of Burrel* and was more than happy to work the sparrows. It took but only a few days, for the younger kids on the block to understand that his authority automatically transferred to his namesake.

The day we moved into our new neighborhood in 1973, the battle for hierarchy and turf began. Percy and Kerry, two kids who lived next-door, caught me on the doorstep that first day and flung nails at me. They drew a few drops of blood, but nothing compared to my first *real* scrap, which came on our second day in the 'hood. Terence, who lived just across the road, held me up, shook me down, and *whipped my ass*.

Terence was older and a lot bigger than me. A great lug of a ten-year-old, he was by nature a bully. He smelled blood the moment I turned up on the street. I was a skinny, cheeky, short kid with the misleadingly benign handle of *Buddy Burrel*. I can see why Terence probably thought: "pushover." He should have sniffed the air a little more carefully though. Maybe he would have caught the heady whiff of my dad's power.

When Burrel Senior was informed (*not* by me, I might add) that Terence had waylaid me, kicked my ass, and stolen my cash, he stormed across the road furious—and fully loaded.

My dad was scary at the best of times, but when he was mad—*really* mad—giants quaked. Terence was quick to grasp the facts of life, and soon he and I developed an understanding based on pure pragmatism and naked self-interest. Along with Kerry, Percy, and Demetrius, another thirsty young local, Terence became a founding member of my neighborhood crew.

It was Wenny, though, who would become my partner in crime, friend, confidant, and collaborator.

Wenny: Act I

Wenny was awesome!

He approached me one day and asked me to put in a word with my dad. My old man—a master of many trades—was well known for being able to produce a superior *natural*, the big, afro-perms that were so popular with blacks at the time. Wenny, a.k.a. Wiz, wanted to make a trade—a *natural* in exchange for a tailored suit of clothes.

I eyed his stylish ensemble: the light gray, pinstripe, tailored suit with big lapels and puffed shoulders; the cool white T-shirt (perfect for muscle flexing); the black, pointy-toed shoes; and the huge "Michael Jackson" hair. I already owned a few nice suits myself, but this was *grown-up* stuff. My dad wore similar uniforms when he went out at night, and though I'd always admired the way he looked, I hadn't realized this was a style a kid like me could wear, too. The trade was done. I got my first taste of *ghetto-chic*, and Wenny and I became fast friends.

Wenny was a short, slight boy, no more than 5'5" even as an adult. He was eleven years old when we met; it was difficult to believe that he was nearly four years older than me. In fact, I was so mature for my years that the age difference was never really noticeable.

We got on like a house on fire. He came from a family of four boys living just down the street, on the corner of Cortez and Lamon. His mom, a hard-working night nurse, and his dad—who'd left home years earlier and worked full-time at a taxicab stand—both gave Wenny a lot of latitude. Pretty much a free agent, Wiz, unlike me, had *no* curfew to keep.

Wenny's three brothers were a mixed bag. Trey was the one I remember most clearly. A few years older than Wiz, though not much taller, Trey had just become a member of the elite Chicago Cadillac Club run by Big Daddy June. We were impressed, largely because he had somehow managed to bluff his way through the club's tough initiation requirements, as the owner of a souped-up, spivved-up Buick.

That was Trey though. Notorious as a *quick-pick* merchant, he'd always expend minimal effort and maximum hot air to get a quick return; an attractive but generally short-sighted strategy. With his sharp threads and swagger, Trey gave the impression of being a real smooth player, but you only had to scratch the surface lightly, to see the wannabe beneath the gloss. Wenny didn't plan on being labeled a fake like his brother.

Trey wasn't an unusual character in our neighborhood. He was just another guy caught up in a typical Catch-22, relentlessly and shamelessly self-promoting, in order to gain respect and station, and then falling into the trap of believing his own bullshit.

Ghetto guys swallow their own propaganda all the time. Buying into whatever image they've created for themselves, they come to believe in their own power and invulnerability—which is, of course, nothing but a mirage. Over time the myth becomes tougher to sustain, and the whole shaky deck of cards has to be shored up with bravado, usually from a bottle, packet, or needle. Such guys burned up their money, merchandise, and credibility, eventually ending up on a treacherous downhill slide toward the penitentiary or a hole in the ground.

I was envious of Wenny's freedom; he envied me my father.

Burrel Senior took a shine to Wiz and his family straight off. He even moved them into the second floor of one of his apartment buildings, just over the road from our house, above a Jamaican weed dealer with whom he did a lot of business.

I never fully understood why there was such a strong bond between Wenny and my dad, although I have some ideas. I believe Burrel Senior liked the fact that Wenny was a born hustler and survivor. I think he saw shades of himself in this sharp, charming, entertaining young man. Perhaps, too, he saw the chance to mold another young protégé in his image, one to whom he could one day entrust chunks of a flourishing business empire.

And have no doubt; Wenny *was* charming. He was the best possible company, even though in reality his sunny persona was just a useful façade that allowed him to get close enough to people to creep under their defenses. Wiz would enter any room with a smile and a joke, and within minutes, everyone there would be eating right out of his hand. No matter if you were child or chief, you'd soon be laughing, back-slapping, and confiding in Wiz as if he were an old friend.

Yes, he was a charmer all right. But he was also *toxic*. Like an iridescent but poisonous snake, he'd charm and disarm. Those hungry eyes of his were *always* watching for an opportunity. If Wenny could find a path to get to you while you were sleeping, he'd make a deadly strike in a moment.

With few morals and little conscience, Wiz was almost entirely driven by personal gain and preservation. Every dirty trick I ever learned, I learned from him. If my old man saw the truth behind the veneer, he didn't say. He treated Wenny like a son and openly approved of the fact that he and I were as thick as thieves. And thieves we most certainly were. There wasn't a hustle we weren't into.

Fresh Greens

A whole new dimension was added to my "domestic" routine in 1974, as the result of Burrel Senior, in partnership with his cousin Charles Selvey, offering an outrageously high amount of cash for a small grocery store on the corner of Keeler and Augusta.

The owners in residence, an elderly couple, had become fearful of living and working in a neighborhood that was often unpredictably violent. Mr. and Mrs. Garcia had already been robbed twice at gunpoint, and eagerly grabbed the chance to retire from the store they'd owned for more than ten years. Dad's offer was accepted, and B&C Grocery was born. The Wilkses became shopkeepers!

By now, my father had bought a number of apartment blocks throughout the area and was renting them out to tenants. These investments gave him equity, a regular rent-roll, and equally important, a number of safe-houses in which to conduct business. Our new acquisition became the jewel in this crown.

I wonder often about my dad's passion for the B&C Grocery. Sure, it was a great front and, on occasion, a useful money laundry. It made money, too. On a good day, the store might take in up to five hundred dollars. It provided handy employment for members of Dad's extended family, including Amy and her cousins. They, along with a host of others, worked an elaborate system of shifts so there was room enough for everyone.

But I believe there were more profound reasons for my father's desire to buy the store, reasons linked to his roots in Mississippi and the deprivations he'd experienced as a child. I think he loved the whole idea of owning a shop stocked with *anything* you might ever need. It was like a little treasure chest, his own personal cache, full of treats he could dip into anytime he wanted.

The store itself was small but sharp, the floor plan designed to optimize return. It boasted a deli at the back, slot machines at the front, and, in-between the two, three rows of shelves stacked high with tins, packets, candy, and all kinds of other tasty treats.

Managing the store added magnitude to the tasks already piling on my eight-year-old shoulders. Now I had to open and close the shop each day and keep it stocked and secure, as well as work the deli. For the most part, I did my job well, with only one or two small mishaps—like the time I nearly sliced off my pinky while flirting and cutting ham at the same time. The only thing running faster than my blood that day was that girl out the door!

I *hated* the early mornings and the hard work required to keep all those shelves fully stocked, but I *loved* the janglin' of keys, hanging off that big fat ring, as I opened up my little domain each day. The kudos of being the only kid in the neighborhood who could boast a store-sized lunchbox, filled with confectionery and cake, was very satisfying. I made sure we were the first to stock all the new candy products and was the envy of every kid for blocks around.

From the ages of eight to sixteen, the store was an essential part of my life. I loved it and loathed it in equal measures.

Player Paradise

I was experiencing a degree of frustration by the time I was eight years old. I had my own hustles going down, but I was still paying daily homage to my dad. He pulled the strings, weighed me down with chores, and handed out *twos and fews* as the mood took him—his level of generosity contingent on his frame of mind.

Bubbles of resentment began to rise to the surface.

I took my resentments into the schoolyard and wreaked havoc at St. Peters, the "nice," private Catholic School Dad had insisted that I attend. As a kid, I may have been a lot of things, but choirboy sure wasn't one of them! I used to douse everyone with holy water at the compulsory masses, and I was the scourge of the playground, fleecing the other kids whenever I got the chance. I was no stranger to truancy. In fact, of the ninety-one days I was enrolled at St. Peters, I played hooky on sixty-three of them. Eventually, the headmaster requested that Dad remove me from his establishment, and put me in the local public school. Dad was furious. I was over the moon!

Burrel Senior was a shrewd man and took steps, in his own way, to dampen these early signs of rebellion. Just before my ninth birthday, he allowed me move into my own apartment in the basement of 4916 West Cortez Street. Nothing short of *playa-paradise,* the space was around 1,300 square feet in area and accommodated two bedrooms, a lounge, a laundry room, and tons of other exciting—and useful—nooks and crannies.

I moved my California King waterbed into the main bedroom and, aping the design my dad had adopted in his bedroom, decorated my room in early American seashore. I hung huge white fishing nets and dozens of dangling seashells on the walls and ceiling. Though more than a little incongruous for a gang-banger's basement pad, the style was, at the time, considered very avant-garde. I'd never actually set eyes on the ocean, and frankly had little inclination to. With the vast expanse of Lake Michigan and its beaches on our doorstep, what more could an ocean *possibly* offer?

It was the finishing touches that made my crib the talk of the neighborhood though, a selection of custom features that had friend and enemy alike drooling with envy. Red, white, and blue marble tiling was laid throughout; the colors chosen with care as a symbol of my patriotism. I was, without irony, genuinely grateful for the free-wheeling economy that offered such great wealth-creation opportunity! Atop these migraine-inducing tiles sat an enormous twelve-person, Jacuzzi tub in the bedroom, and a slick, red velvet DJ booth in the lounge.

It didn't take long before the "clubhouse" became *the* neighborhood place to be. Sounds of music and laughter would drift up from this subterranean den almost every night. We'd hang out, chill, shake drugs and take drugs, drink syrup, count money, mess with girls, and *step*. Stepping was the dance of the moment. Rhythmic and synchronized, it was almost hypnotic and people loved to do it as a way of freeing their spirits and minds from the world lying in wait outside the walls.

The memories I have of preparing for parties are happy ones: soaking and steaming, primping and preening, strutting my stuff in front of the mirror. I was just a cocky kid with the world at my feet. Life was good.

When my dad was around, we mostly listened to grass-roots reggae. I loved the island sound and could listen to Bob Marley, Jacob Miller, and Eeky Mouse for hours. But after Dad left the room, Barry White was my main man! Much as I admired my father, when it came to *chicks*, Barry was in a class of his own. If you're going to learn something new, then study with *the master.*

Every night as I made ready for a wild evening in the clubhouse, Barry's music would blast through my apartment. I was word perfect in every song. Singing along boisterously, I'd poke out my chest and play to imaginary TV cameras: "Just can't get enough of your love, baby . . ."

I thought I was as cool as iced lemonade!

My pad was the greatest. It had both a front and back entrance, which meant I could tell my parents I was going to bed for the night, but actually slip out the back door and go about my business. I'd pile some cushions under the covers, in case someone popped their face in, and head into the night.

> " *I covered up for Burrel so often. He was always—I mean always—in terrible trouble with his father. It just seemed to build up, layer on layer on layer. I spent half my life trying to smooth things over and the other half holding my breath waiting for the explosion.* "
> —Gloria Wilks

Mom put in a full shift at the hospital every day and would often take on a few extra overtime hours, so she would usually get home quite late in the evening. On arriving she'd prepare and eat dinner, downing a couple of pink champagnes while she was at it. Afterwards she'd put up her feet, enjoy another tipple, and soon would be gently snoring from the depths of the armchair, neither knowing, nor caring what I was up to.

The old man was away from home much of the time, but on those occasions when he wasn't, he sometimes used my crib for his own conferences. Thankfully, this didn't happen too often, and for the most part, I was king in my own private castle.

Having my own apartment meant more to me than the convenience of a space in which to live and party. It represented freedom and power.

I'd hardly acknowledged my childhood years as I vaulted over them. With tens of thousands of dollars stashed in various corners of my pad, I was already wealthy and mature *way* beyond my years. I'd experienced things most grown men *never would or ever should.* I partied, played, labored, learned, and sampled just about every narcotic substance known to man. My ambition and aspiration, vigorous forces both, felt unnaturally constrained in this still-small body.

Rushing headlong down the path to adulthood, I was eager to forge my own way and clamored to be given free rein.

CHAPTER FOUR

Four The Hard Way

1976–1977 (Age 9–10 Years)

"Fast-Guns" and Hard Heads

I INHERITED MUCH FROM MY DAD INCLUDING MORE *MOXIE* THAN ANY MAN HAS THE RIGHT TO EXPECT. It was when those aspects of my character—being highly resourceful and virtually fearless—were blended with an energy that was all but *nuclear,* that extraordinary things happened!

"The problem with skateboarding," I said to Rickey one day, "is that by the time you're goin' fast enough, it's time to stop. What we have to do is figure how to hit the ground runnin'." After some serious discussion, we agreed that the best way to achieve this result would be to propel ourselves out of the back of a fast-moving vehicle.

We'd been hitching rides on lurching truck tailgates for some time now. Precariously balanced on skateboards and skates, we'd hang on for grim death, as they trundled along, towing us in their wake.

Based on these earlier trials, we selected a local UPS delivery van as a suitable launch pad. As the driver went about his business, hopping in and out to make deliveries, we snuck on board. The truck set off again, picking up speed. I watched the road flow by beneath its wheels. When we hit a speed of 20 m.p.h. or so, I launched myself off the far wall with as much force as I could muster, roaring toward the open flap at the back, with Rickey revving up behind me.

The road rushed up with the speed of an express train. The impact was *skull-cracking*. Careening out of control, the wheels of my skateboard buckled and I hit the asphalt with sickening force, somersaulting several times over. My head whip-lashed, bouncing off the rock-hard surface with such an almighty crack that for a second everything went black and the world stopped turning.

On coming to, seconds later, I thought I must have split my skull from ear to ear, but miraculously I surfaced with only a golf ball-sized lump on the back of my head. Rickey—*smart* boy—decided not to jump. If further proof of my hardheadedness was required, I sure delivered it that day! Left with a permanent bony protuberance, I wear it today as a tangible reminder of the roulette games this foolish boy played with his life.

I inherited other traits in spades from my dad, too, notably self-confidence, ambition, and pride. More than anything I aspired to be him. I hungered to be the big guy pulling the strings, not the little guy doing the dancing; the one making the rules, not following them. My father had given me all the tools I'd need for the job.

Before hitting double digits, I was skimming from my father's takings every other night, pocketing two or three grand at a time. With Wenny's encouragement, I began going back to the house more frequently, when Dad was out, to raid his safe.

Each time I robbed him, I justified it to myself with the thin argument that I was never paid properly for all the hours I put in at home and at the store. My own street endeavors were already generating tons of ready cash, which I stockpiled in various places, so I didn't *need* my dad's money. But by now, I was too hooked on the accompanying adrenaline-kick of pulling one over on my old man, to give it up.

An ambitious student of the streets, Wiz had been out there for years, with little or no fatherly restraint, hanging around the big shots and the *fast guns*. His aspirations went way beyond the chump change we were collecting from our small-scale scams. Wenny couldn't wait to get into the *real* game.

When he saw the steady supply of weed, and eventually cocaine and dope, that flowed through my father's hands and was available to us, he could hardly contain himself. Soon, with my complicity, we were taking product to the streets.

Dancing with Drugs

Throughout this book, you'll come face-to-face with the unpalatable subject of narcotics, their consumption, and their sale. The *culture* around narcotics is complex and complicated, and I'm not looking to justify, excuse, or explain my participation. I can only share my story.

Drugs were an indisputable part of my life: an immutable, nonnegotiable fact of my childhood. From the time I could walk, I was immersed in the twilight world of narcotics. I viewed them as legitimate *currency* and spent little—if any—of my early years debating the morality of my actions.

Many guys in the neighborhood, Wenny and myself included, already consumed high volumes of high-potency medication, easily available from any number of *syrup shops*, over-the-counter at stores and pharmacies, or through illegal prescriptions.

If guys in the ghetto were not popping pills or dissolving their teeth and guts with cough syrup, they were downing alcohol. They'd drink anything they could get their hands on, as long as it *worked*. A favorite gang tipple called Blood was made from a combination of white port and strawberry Kool-Aid. At one point, before narcotics flooded the inner cities, wine consumption was more pervasive on the streets than drugs. The logic went: alcohol was readily available, whereas you had to hustle all day to get a fix, and *that* took time away from doing *business*.

To us, dealing in narcotics didn't seem so different from trading in syrup, pills, and mouthwash. We saw ourselves as *contemporary* medicine men. I didn't consider the people who bought drugs to be victims. They were customers. I didn't view those who consumed drugs as *wounded*. I assumed they, like me, could walk away any time they chose. I was a user but didn't see myself as a junkie. I rationalized that getting high was really no different from getting drunk.

Ultimately, I believed it was not *what* you did that harmed you, but how excessively you did it—and *that* was simply a matter of personal choice, wasn't it? As a kid, I had little grasp that few people were gifted with the strength required to say "no" and that it takes a *rare* person to walk away from the life-sapping, soul-sucking, stranglehold of narcotic addiction.

With almost limitless supplies of merchandise flowing through Burrel Senior's channels, like floodwater through a storm drain, we started rolling. We took it to street corners, fire hydrants, front porches, and gathering points—wherever we could put a spot down. We started with nickel bags, and created pyramid sales and distribution channels. If we couldn't control the location directly, we'd *squeeze* someone else's spot for a slice of the take.

Paying about six hundred bucks for a pound of good grass, we'd spilt it into small bags, selling it to middlemen or *runners* for around eighteen hundred dollars. Even after taking their cut—usually around 20 percent—off the top, our markup was still close to 100 percent, doubling our investment. We were buying in bulk, so our profits were substantial.[3]

The Hell Henchmen

By now, we were a tight unit of four, overseeing a rapidly expanding street crew. Day to day, Wiz would kick it with Demetrius, and I'd either hang with Terence or take my own road. We all agreed on one thing: we needed an *identity*.

It was time to align our outfit with one of the many street gangs operating throughout the West Side. Wiz and I initially decided to call our outfit the *Junior Hell Henchman*. I'd heard tell of the Henchmen, and thought the name had a cool ring to it. We formalized our new affinity by having the name stitched, in pink suede, on the back of our denim jackets.

Riding up on the Henchmen, on choppers and skateboards, we soon made a shocking discovery. They were *white*. Predominantly a supremacist group, the Henchmen, it transpired, had strong Ku Klux Klan associations! *Rapidly* shifting allegiance, we became the Demon Love Crew

---

3. Gangs are a major economic force in Chicago, with profit estimates anywhere from $500 million to a billion, or around 1 percent of GDP. For a fascinating glimpse into the economics of drug dealing, read Steven D. Levitt and Stephen J. Dubner, *Freakonomics* (William Morrow, 2005). Also recommended is a visit to the *Chicago Sun Times* archives.

for a while, then the Illinois Players, and subsequently the YBO—the Yates Boys Organization—an alliance with a crew of Puerto Ricans.

Eventually though, by the time I was nine years old, we found a more permanent home as part of the Cicero Insane Vice Lords, the CIVLs.

Chicago Street Gangs

Chicago's black street gangs, of which there are several identifiable *families*—the Vice Lords, the Disciples, and the El Rukns, formerly known as the Blackstone Rangers—were born in the early 1960s. At that time, they were mostly ill-defined groups of young kids battling it out over turf.

Throughout the sixties, the decade in which I was born, street gangs had striven to achieve a degree of organization and respectability. The latter part of the decade witnessed some pretty radical social experiments. Funded in part by government and charitable grants—*a hand up, not a handout*—street gangs formed a number of legitimate social and economic organizations. Some optimists even viewed them as a possible answer to bettering and protecting crime-sodden Chicago neighborhoods.

In 1967, the Conservative Vice Lords were incorporated as a non-profit organization. They opened a number of small businesses including a restaurant; "Teen-Town"; an Afro-American heritage shop; and Tastee Freez, an ice cream parlor. Rumor had it there were a few other ideas that never got off the ground, including a venture into cosmetics with Sammy Davis Jr.[4]

When they chose to do so, gangs could use their power positively. During the devastating street riots of 1968, following the murder of Martin Luther King Jr., the Disciples protected their South Side territory. The Vice Lords' West Side heartland, in contrast, was plundered and razed.

But it all came to naught. In the late sixties, Mayor Richard Daley declared "war on gangs." By the time Wenny and I joined the Vice Lords in 1976—at ages twelve and nine, respectively—any veneer of legitimacy had long gone; betrayed, some might say, by a cynical administration.

---

4. *A Nation of Lords: The Autobiography of The Vice Lords* (Waveland Press Inc., 1992) by David Dawley is an unusual book written by a young, white New Englander. Dawley lived in Chicago, among the infamous Vice Lord leadership, during a turbulent period of their evolution in the sixties. This is a tough, often brutal perspective, of a world seen through the eyes of the gang members themselves, and follows this gang's struggle for identity.

There's irony in the tale though. Legacies of this short flirtation with respectability included greatly strengthened strategic capability and robust operational infrastructure, both essential assets for a street gang to flourish in the new *big business* realities of narcotics trafficking.

The Nation of Lords

At about the time I became a Vice Lord, the city's gangs split into two main groupings known as the *People* and the *Folks*. This division into families came about as a means of reducing intergang friction in prisons, and establishing some sort of unity and order. The People and Folks were actually loose alliances of multiple factions. Both families boasted charters, codes, hierarchies, and strongly emblematic identities.

The Folks included black, white, and Hispanic gangs—the Black Disciples, Simon City Royals, Latin Eagles, Spanish Cobras, Imperial Disciples, and Latin Disciples among them. They adopted a six-point star emblem and *identified* to the right—which meant they either wore caps with brims skewed in that direction or turned up the right leg of their trousers. Their colors were black and blue.

On the other side of the fence were the People, also known as the Nation of Lords, the *Nation* for short. The Vice Lords, Latin Kings, and El Rukns created this alliance to counter the strength of the Folks. Their colors were black and gold, or black and red. Running under the five-point star and half moon pennant—a flag strongly influenced by Islamic religious symbolism—they *identified* to the left. Members of the People often wore long black cloaks.

Today these alliances hold little weight, but during the late seventies and early eighties, they played a significant role in defining territorial boundaries, enforcing street-law, and settling disputes, which could be brought before a *governing* body for mediation. None of this stopped the brawling, shooting, inter-faction rivalry, and retribution, but it did provide an organizational framework, a point of reference, something totally lacking today.

As whites were marginalized, they moved from the black heartlands, following economic opportunity out of the ghetto. Moving away wasn't a viable option for most blacks. Left with no place to go, black-on-black, family versus family, and intra-family feuding flared.

Same Trunk, Different Branches

The Vice Lords can be traced back to the 1950s and are, in fact, the oldest street gang in Chicago history. Formed in the Illinois State Training Center for Boys, this small "club" became a fully fledged street gang when members returned to their Lawndale neighborhoods and began to organize.

Soon, it was hard to keep track of the number of crews running under the five-point star and half moon. The Conservatives, the Unknowns, the Ambrose, the Enforcers, the Black Orpheus, the Stones, the Travelers, the Latin Kings, the Four Corner Hustlers, and the Cicero Insanes were just a few of more than twenty splinter groups that had come to life by the seventies.

Many gang members were recruited in County Jail or the pen. It was another of those Catch-22s. You'd do wrong, get caught, and while doing time, learn how to do more wrong, but on a much greater scale and in a more organized manner. Many kids went behind bars for misdemeanors and emerged as criminals. The prisons eventually became the operational headquarters for a lot of gangs, but in my day, the action was still very much on the streets.[5]

Members pledged allegiance to their chief and respect to a number of symbols. For us Vice Lords, a pair of dice and the Playboy bunny represented that we were *playas*. There were other signs, too. The top hat signified shelter; the cane, strength; the white glove, purity; and a martini (or champagne) glass, conservatism or propriety.[6]

---

5. One of the best illustrations of this point is to be found in the story of Larry Hoover, infamous leader of the Gangster Disciples. The GDs are probably one of the largest and most highly organized street gangs in the U.S. (estimated thirty thousand members in Chicago, but active in thirty-five states). An admirer of Capone, Hoover modeled the GD organization on the Syndicate/Outfit, and micromanaged the organization from a low security prison, while serving a 150–200 year jail term. In 1995, a federal indictment for "conspiracy to conduct a criminal enterprise" (Operation Headache), resulted in conviction and a federal, "super-max" security sentence. Link to http://members.aol.com/gangdigest/journal.html to read "The Impact of the Federal Prosecution of the Gangster Disciples," a paper written by George W. Knox PhD, director of the National Gang Crime Research Center, for some fascinating details on the organization, and copies of gang communiqués.

6. Alex Kotlowitz in his highly recommended work, *There Are No Children Here: The Story of Two Boys Growing Up in the Other America* (Anchor Books, 1992), does a nice job of explaining key aspects of Chicago black gang structure, protocols, and emblems, and in exploring the harsh, often tragic repercussions pervasive gang presence and pressure can wreak on young lives. Link to www.ngcrc.com/ngcrc/page13.htm for a paper by George W. Knox (NGCRC) who explores GD emblems and symbolism.

Tattoos

I got my first tattoo at eight; it was a top hat and cane imprinted on my left knuckle, along with the initials CIVL (Cicero Insane Vice Lords). A playboy bunny, on my right arm, followed that, and at eleven years old, I had a heart and cross stamped onto my left forearm. By this time, I was running tight, with a small, inner-circle of guys, and we branded this little clique-within-a-clique, *The Stone Brothers*. The cross was our mark.

But tattoos are much more than the rubber-stamp of gang membership. They are a way of making a personal statement, a unique reaffirmation of identity.

As I grew older, the symbols I chose to ink into my skin were reflective of my evolution and growth. Like illustrations in the book of my life, they were less about *belonging* and more about *affirmation*. I never took this act of placing a seal of ownership on my body lightly. My marks are individual, precious, and represent milestones on the road along which I walked.

CHAPTER FIVE

The Italian Connection

1978 (Age 11 Years)

Ol' Skool Original Gangsta

WENNY AND I JOINED THE VICE LORDS WITH OUR OWN CREW IN TOW, so there were no membership rituals or entry-level rankings for us. Under the roof of the Cicero Insanes, we were given due respect and recognition from the start. We continued to reinforce our status and, over the next few years, steadily ramped up our business.

We were now several hundred strong on the street, if you included runners and go-betweens, and were moving high volumes of weed and coke. We continued to grow distribution; sourcing merchandise from new suppliers, as well as from my father.

Chicago is a critical distribution center for narcotics. As one of the most strategically situated cities in the U.S. with the largest and busiest airport, the city has always been a major global hub.[7] By now, we were dealing with Jamaicans, Mexicans, Puerto Ricans, and Colombians. There

---

7. For a wealth of information on the drug trade, including facts, figures, stats, and trafficking volumes and patterns, check out the DEA Web site: www.DEA.gov.

was no limit to the amount of *merch* we could buy. Our only constraint was how much we could sell.

We created new channels wherever we could. We also opened a number of smoke houses, learned how to freebase, and doubled our business each month. But we were sampling the goods, too, and slowly but surely, succumbing to addiction ourselves.

Even though Wiz and I were still officially *shorties,* the forces with which we were now aligned and the volume of merchandise we shifted put us on an equal footing with the most powerful gang leadership in the area. By now I was spending significant time managing my assets out on the streets, and took to hanging regularly with some of the older chiefs—the real *original gangsters* (OGs). Most of these guys were in their late twenties and thirties, and were *for-real, no-messin', ol' skool playas.* Our relationships were unique.

It wasn't unusual to see kids my age, in and around gangs. For years, youngsters ranging in age from six to thirteen had been used as bagmen. These *pee-wees* often did the dirty work, too. Rationalizing that they faced only Juvenile court if caught, the gang leadership gambled these kids' futures away. They paid them to take the rap if they got caught and promised rich rewards when the system finally spat them out. But, of course, by the time they'd gone through the system, most had been "spoilt" and there was no going back.

And it wasn't always a low-risk strategy for the chiefs either. These younger kids could be *bad little muthafuckas.* Hungry to build their names, they often lacked any moral framework for their actions. Like the child-soldiers you hear about in other countries, these scraps of kids could be pointed in any direction, instructed to *kill,* and would hurtle forward, as lethal as any Scud. Just watch your back though, because the next target was just as likely to be *you.*[8]

Wenny and I liked hanging with the older guys, and we were powerful and precocious enough to hold our own in their elevated company. In return, they treated us with respect, as equals.

Killing time on street corners, we shot the breeze, did business, and watched the world go by. On more than a few occasions, I'd noticed an

---

8. For additional perspective, read David Dawley's *A Nation of Lords* (Waveland Press Inc., 1992) and Alex Kotlowitz's *There Are No Children Here* (Anchor Books, 1991).

older, well-heeled guy driving slowly down Madison Boulevard. Nothing moving in our territory ever slipped by, without being scanned and cataloged, but it seemed pretty clear this guy wasn't trying to keep a low profile. He *was looking* for attention.

In his sixties, he drove a sleek, powder-blue Rolls Royce Silver Shadow, with dark blue leather interior. Whenever we saw him, he'd be wearing a sharp jacket, a fedora, and smoked-black, almost impenetrable, shades. This was a guy whose attitude needed no translation. We recognized him as one of us, a chief, and as it turned out, no ordinary chief. This man was nothing less than a *legend*.

As we congregated at different spots along Madison or Augusta, we noticed him driving by with increasing frequency. Sometimes he'd acknowledge us with a casual salute. Then one warm April day, that powder-blue, winged angel purred up beside us, drifting to rest as softly as a feather settling. The car was a showstopper all right, but *all* eyes were on the man behind the wheel.

Tony "Big Tuna" Accardo

Chests puffed and mouths poked, we tried to inject the right mix of menace and nonchalance into our demeanor, as the driver heaved himself out of the car.

He introduced himself as Tony. A compact man with a dark complexion and weathered, fleshy face, he commanded instant deference. Standing in front of us was none other than Tony "Big Tuna" Accardo, the longstanding boss of the Chicago Outfit, and one of the most powerful and successful mobsters in the history of La Cosa Nostra.[9]

Accardo, a graduate of Prohibition Era gangland, was infamous. He was an OG with a reputation for a clear head and iron fists. He'd run with the big boys back in the twenties and thirties—coming to the attention of Capone himself—and took over leadership of the Outfit in 1946.

We knew of him, of course. He'd started mob life as an enforcer and was, by all accounts, pitiless. There was talk that Tony had been at Al

---

9. One of the most comprehensive and interesting profiles of Tony Accardo (and the Outfit) is to be found in Gus Russo's, *The Outfit: The Role of Chicago's Underworld in the Shaping of Modern America* (Bloomsbury, 2003), but for a fascinating photographic journey, check out John Binder's, *The Chicago Outfit* (Arcadia Publishing, 2004).

Capone's side in some of the Prohibition Era Mob wars. His other handle—
Tony "Joe Batters" Accardo—was based on a rumor that he wielded a
baseball bat, with fatal results, during some of those confrontations.

Shortly after we met, his reputation was sealed once and for all. In
January 1977, prior to our meeting, his home in River Forest had been
robbed, while he was out of town on the West Coast. In an act of *extraordinary*, reckless stupidity, a bunch of hapless burglars unknowingly signed
their own death warrants. If they'd assumed Tony had lost his teeth, they
were horribly wrong, and the revenge wreaked was callous, even by ghetto,
battle-hardened standards. Tony allegedly put a hit out on the perpetra-
tors, and over a year later, in a murder spree spanning eight weeks, each
of the seven alleged culprits turned up dead. They had been violently
and, in several cases, tortuously dispatched.

Even before this, we'd heard rumors of his ruthlessness and reach,
but in reality the Outfit's operations seemed worlds apart from our West
Side turf. We were cocky, young, black men in our home territory. We
thought we ruled the world, so when Tony "Big Tuna" Accardo appeared
on our doorstep, we were more curious than impressed.

Negotiations Commence

I clearly remember my first impressions of Tony. Born in 1906, he was then
in his late sixties. He was a swarthy, first-generation Italian with gray hair,
still-wavy, swept back high on his forehead and slicked down with some
kind of grease. Although he wasn't fat, he had the jowls of a heavier-set man,
a prominent nose, and keen, pouched eyes under thick brows.

His clothes reeked of money and style, all flowing lines of cashmere
and silk, cut as only the Italians know how. His was the demeanor of a
man of power, a man intimidated by nothing—least of all this crew of
truculent gang-bangers in their flashy ghetto suits and diamonds. We
made sure he didn't miss the fact that we were carrying iron, but he
wasn't fazed.

He spoke first. "You boys represent this 'hood." It was a statement not
a question.

As usual, I jumped right in. "Wha's goin' down, man?"

He swiveled and took off his shades, the keenness of his gaze homing in on me. If he was surprised to see a preteen kid taking the lead, it didn't show on his face.

"I wanna sit down with you boys," he said bluntly, "and soon. There's things goin' down that need handling."

He was right, of course.

Some of the nastier activities that flourished on the West Side had inevitably bled into neighboring areas. There was only one block—Austen—separating us from the manicured gardens and immaculate mansions of the village suburbs of Oak Park and River Forest. It was altogether too tempting for some.

Young blacks had been crossing the line from Austen into Oak Park and River Forest, with increasing frequency and committing "hit-and-run" crimes. Those activities were escalating in severity and recklessness. What had started as a small problem—local kids having their bikes and skateboards wrestled from them—was mounting. The incursions became bolder by the week. Recently, raiders had begun hitting the larger houses, even while the owners were at home. Locking their terrified victims in the trunks of their own cars, they'd ransack the house stripping it of any portable valuables. This practice was known, not surprisingly, as *trunkin'* (as distinct from *trunk music,* the somewhat more deadly mob practice of leaving bodies in car trunks).

But River Forest and Oak Park were the residential heartland of the Outfit. Tony Accardo had settled there years ago, as had previous Outfit bosses—guys like Paul Ricca and Sam Giancana. In fact, there were so many mobsters and their extended families living in the area that it had become known as "the home of the hoods."[10] When one of Tony's crew became a victim of a *trunkin'*, Tony decided to put a stop to these travesties, right now. They had begun to hit too close to home.

Wenny, a few other leaders, and I—eight of us in all—met with Tony for an initial sit-down a few days later, at a bustling breakfast joint called Grandmas in Oak Park. Over stacks of pancakes and plates of eggs, we opened discussions. The conversation went well enough to pave the way for a second, more serious, meeting to take place at Tony's home, a week

---

10. Binder, *The Chicago Outfit.*

or two later. Word was circulated, and five of the most influential West Side chiefs convened for the next powwow.

Wenny: Act II

Tony's home on North Ashland was a relatively modest but nicely appointed corner house. Low-rise in design, I estimated it covered maybe 3,000 square feet or so, although I never saw the full layout. Tony had moved to this address in 1963 from a far more opulent, twenty-two-room mansion on Franklin Avenue, just around the corner.

The Franklin Avenue house was an ornate, flamboyant piece of work. It allegedly boasted all the trimmings that would have deeply impressed us: huge vaulted rooms, an indoor swimming pool with a garden on its roof, a gun and trophy room, a huge black onyx bathtub, a fully stocked library, a two-lane bowling alley, and enough beds and baths for a small army, or a *very* large, extended family.

In contrast, Ashland Avenue was disappointingly modest for a man of Tony's stature and power. We'd been hoping to see some flashy, over-the-top, Italian opulence, but these days Tony kept a low profile. It was one of his trademarks. So we settled, with an air of anticlimax, around a large oval table in the basement meeting room. All the *master-links* were in attendance. Between us, we could speak for the majority of the West Side—on that day at least.

Conversation was lively and loud. Both vintage cognac and gin—Tony's drink of choice—flowed freely, as we got down to the business of the day. It was under cover of this well-oiled din that Wenny quietly slipped away from the group, ostensibly to use the bathroom, and just as quickly slipped up the basement stairs to the first floor and its bedrooms.

He rifled through drawers and bedside cabinets, pocketing a gold watch and diamond ring before heading back downstairs to the bathroom. There, he proceeded to lay down a noisy eight-track of flushing toilets, running faucets, and crashing doors before rejoining the group nonchalantly enough for none of us to notice anything amiss.

But, of course, there were no secrets in the house of a guy who used to hang with Al Capone and little did Wiz, or we, know, that every inch of that house—even the inside of the bathroom—was *wired*! There may have been as many as sixty or seventy cameras covering every nook and cranny of Tony's domain. This was *not* a man given to trusting people. Wenny's every action had been captured by an all-seeing, all-hearing army of winking camera lenses.

The meeting continued exuberantly, and we debated the issue at hand with gusto—put a bunch of *street niggas* in a room and you're guaranteed a ruckus! We were talking over each other, bickering, arguing, wrangling, and generally having a *good* time. In due course, we settled on the terms of an agreement, or treaty, that would stem the flow of West Side renegades toward Tony's middle class, suburban territory.

Tony stood up and moved across the room to a wooden cabinet set against the far wall. He opened one of its drawers, took out some bundles of cash, and handed them to us to divide as we saw fit. All in all, there was about $300,000 to share: a healthy enough windfall.

"This in *not* protection money," he emphasized. "I'm just giving you something to *work with*."

He paused and looked witheringly at each of us in turn. "We don't fuck around with *narcotics* in my family, but whatever you do with this money is up to you. Just stop these guys from coming into my neighborhood, *bothering* people."

It seemed like a fair trade. We left the meeting with a few extra dollars in hand and a sense that the "Italian Connection" could prove to be a fruitful one. The day following this somewhat unusual convention, however, I received an unexpected call. It was Tony: "Burrel, I want you to come out here to talk with me, and I want you to come by yourself."

Encore

Clearly, something was up. I told Tony I'd be there and be there alone, by five that afternoon. To make sure my back was covered, I informed Wiz and a couple of my crew, exactly what was going down. Wenny, having a far better idea than I as to what it was *really* all about, blanched as white as Wonderbread. He mustered as many arguments as he could, to dissuade me from going, and when they failed, played the *brotherhood* card.

"You can't trust no *muthafuckin'* Italians, man," he spluttered. "Don' you go flying solo now, bro'. Us niggas gotta stick together."

But I was deeply intrigued by the call and ever the optimist, could only speculate that Tony had something big to put on the table. *No way* was Wenny going to divert me from this appointment.

Tony met me at the door, a bodyguard by his side. His demeanor was far different from the day before. His countenance displayed hard edges that hadn't been evident yesterday, the lines etched more deeply, the eyes colder.

He didn't mince words: "Come with me. I've got something you need to see."

He sure did. There, caught like a rabbit in the headlights, in glorious if grainy full action, was *Wenny the Sneak Thief*!

We viewed the video footage, both silent, Tony's muscleman sitting quietly, and ominously, behind us. Tony poured a glass of champagne, watched the bubbles rise for a second or two, and sipped carefully as he watched the black and white images of Wenny, unsuspectingly starring in his movie debut, tonight's production of armchair theater.

And he was a bad, B-movie actor! Exaggerating all his gestures, Wiz peered through a crack in the bathroom door before self-consciously slithering out of the room and tiptoeing up the stairs. As this act of treachery unfolded, it was hard for me to sit still. It cut deeply. I burned with fury and embarrassment. We'd come to the house of a *giant*, and Wenny had behaved like a *minnow*.

The impromptu home movie came to an end, and Tony turned to me. If he saw an eleven-year-old kid in front of him, he sure didn't show it.

"Look at this *fuckin' shit*," he seethed. "I give you niggas three hundred grand of my own *goddamn* money, and *this* is how you repay me?"

He sipped more champagne, swallowing deeply. It seemed like I could hear it going all the way down.

"You spoke up for this nigga, Burrel. *You* brought him into my house. Tell me why I should even let you leave here alive?"

I looked straight back at him with an arrogance that must have been hard for an *ol' skool* guy like Tony to comprehend, and even harder for him to swallow. I was a cocky little black kid, giving as good as I got.

"Because you're smart, Tony," I said.

I went on to tell him what he already knew: that if anything happened to me those guys he called *niggas* would swarm across Austen like roaches

44

Here I am at eight years old. Angelic smile, sharp suit, and already a *playa*, partying the nights away in my own basement pad!

① Little did Mom know what was in store for us all, when she held me on her knee as a sweet little two-year-old.

② A little man even at three.

③ Jackie, Marcel, and me: all budding performers. Marcel's "natural" is stand out!

④ I took good care of my baby brother, Marcel, when I wasn't landing him in deep trouble, that is!

① Dad and his green thumb! This was a different kind of gardening . . .

② Dad and me, many years later. Two peas in a pod. We're the best of friends today.

③ My wonderful, gentle mom. A truly lovely lady.

① Clockwise starting from top left: Little Red, Googie, Kendell, Jitterbug, and [ ] at age thirteen. We were all CIVLs (Cicero Insane Vice Lords) and our salute [ ] two fingers to the right temple—translates as "insane to the brain."

② Here I am at age fifteen, with Big Daddy June (right) and Rayford, both ma[ ] gang chiefs. Big Daddy was also head of the elite Cadi-Club.

③ At seventeen, with Ice Ray, an ex-kingpin from the South Side. Notice the [ ] I'm carrying. The bulge is cash, around $500,000 in C-Notes.

❶ Ray Ray, Wenny, and me. Wenny named his Uzi, Izola, after his first love, and used to carry it everywhere, covered by a white towel. Twenty years after this picture was taken, Ray, chief of the Four Corner Hustlers, is facing life in the penitentiary.

❷ Money, a topflight *playa* from the South Side, and me. Notice the medallion I'm wearing. Solid gold, embossed with a Taurus bull made from diamonds, this was real bling!

Doctor was one of
...tacts, operating out
...square-foot "herbal

...and the infamous
...ty (currently
...y-five years). Pam
...love.

Willie Mason, a major West Side operator famous for his spending habits. Willie once bought three Mercedes in one week: a 560 SEL on Monday, an SL 380 on Wednesday, and a 560 SEC on Saturday.

❶ Wenny and me, brothers in all but blood.

❷ Sharper than a double–edged razor!

❸ On fire, and ready for Saturday night. The bulge in Wiz's pocket is his spending money.

❹ R&R. Rhythm and rollers. I can still spin and twirl with the

I'm nineteen years old and have left the game but not the glitz. I was back and forth to Beverly Hills, and having a ball. The Gucci ensemble: suit, shoes, and bag were as low-key as me! In fact, shoes like this are back on the market today.

This tight "Inner Circle" wielded tremendous street power.
Top row: Myself at fifteen, CIVL chief; Duck, Conservative Vice Lords
(suffered mental damage from PCP); Big Sam, CIVL; Sam McKay: chief of
the Souls (in the penitentiary for sixty-five years); Sam's right-hand man,
Sosa; Codeine, CIVL (the man who beat me out of $10 million and eventu-
ally became a preacher); Willy Cage, chief of the Undertakers (murdered).
Front row: F.C., CIVL (crippled after a shooting); Twin, Souls (dead); and
Eddie, no known affiliation.

man and steel.

I had just left Tony Accardo's house to attend my "coming out" party, a bash to celebrate my leaving the street game. I'm with General (right) and Kenny Steel. I was definitely feeling "Rat Pack" that night!

at a garbage strike. They'd overrun the whole area. Life as he knew it today, in this elegant neighborhood, would be all but over.

Tony's eyes narrowed, and he considered me some more. When he spoke again, it was a little wearily; he was nothing if not pragmatic.

"That little *muthufuckin'* bastard! I knew I couldn't trust him as soon as I saw him. But let me tell you, Burrel, you're a for real guy, and that's one nigga you don't need. He's a snake. He's got no values, no honor, and no sense."

He looked hard at me again. "Watch out, Burrel. He's going to be the death of you one day."

I knew he was wrong, of course. Wiz and I may have differences, but our bond went deep. In the ghetto, brotherhood is not taken lightly. I wonder, though, through some gift of foresight, if Wiz had glimpsed the dreadful fate of the poor fools who previously broke into Tony's home, would he still have robbed him?

My guess is yes. He couldn't stop himself. Wenny had balls of brass and an almost *delusional* sense of his own impunity. He'd never yet encountered a situation he couldn't talk his way out of.

The first time he did, it would be far too late.

It Wasn't Me!

Wenny denied everything, of course.

For obvious reasons, Tony wouldn't give me the surveillance tape, and even when I told Wenny I'd *seen* him with my own *two* eyes, caught red-handed on tape, he still denied everything without flinching.

"That fuckin' Italian's lying. He's just fulla shit, man. Who you goin' believe anyway, me or a fuckin' *wop*?"

In that moment, I saw with clarity, just how completely amoral Wenny was. I'd always known him to be unscrupulous, but somehow this awareness was tempered, by his disarming personal charm. It felt good to bask in the glow of Wenny's friendship. Any notion of potential treachery was pushed firmly away, until it gleamed dull and impotent, somewhere in a corner of my mind, like a coin lost in the cushions of a chair. Wenny was a dangerous friend to have. The packaging was attractive, but the heart was missing.

After the "Wenny Incident," Tony wouldn't deal with anyone but me.

He told me he liked my style, my character, and my spunkiness. He felt we could work together. This was another of those watershed moments in my street "career" that was to set me apart from others.

Over the next few years, Tony "Joe Batters" took me under his wing, giving me unique access to himself and a privileged glimpse into the inner circles of the Outfit. My relationship with Tony would change my life. Over the years, as advisor, mentor, and instructor, he would teach me invaluable lessons about myself that I *never* wanted to learn.

CHAPTER SIX

Putting Up The Factory While On The Job

1979–1980 (Ages 12–13 Years)

Business Flourishes

By the time I was twelve, Wiz and I were each making more than a $100,000 a week from the streets, to which we'd add the money skimmed from my dad. But still, we hustled all day and sometimes all night. We worked every angle possible, from playground protection to carboosting to stickups and pickpocketing.

We'd head into neighboring territories to "work," sometimes commuting more than a hundred miles. On Cortez Street, we were vigilantes—woe betide anyone who brought trouble into our front-yard—but outside our own streets, we were *pillagers,* not *protectors*.

My father had little idea how profitable our business had become, since he'd let me loose to work the small fry, four years earlier. He continued to receive large drug shipments that he plastic-wrapped, stashed, and sold, but generally he didn't keep close track of the daily ebb and flow of merchandise. The stuff moved in and out by the truckload, and sometimes our house felt like loading dock and train station combined. It was easy to obscure the amount of product we sold direct.

We'd also opened new channels to a number of heavyweight suppliers and were becoming less dependent, by the day, on Burrel Senior's merchandise. Drugs of all kinds were easily available to us. They flowed into the inner cities from South America, Cuba, Mexico, and increasingly from Asia. No, supply wasn't a problem. We had our fingers in all the necessary pies.

Once one emerges as a significant cog in the narcotics business machine, a mile-long queue forms outside your door. Guys, arms full, proffer anything you could possibly want—for the right price, of course.

I'd learned early on: there was virtue in disguising your hand at all times, and we kept our independent arrangements secret from Dad, even as we expanded operations. Our street team grew to more than two thousand strong, but to my dad, I was still strictly small-time, dealing ounces on the streets to the little guys he couldn't be bothered with.

It was also around this time that I adopted Jamaican patois as my preferred "business" language. The advantages of using this distinctive dialect were many: I was already fluent, having learned it from my dad who learned it from his buddy, Joe; it confused the hell out of people; and unless you were familiar with it—as were many of the guys with whom I did business—it was all but *impenetrable*.

The police had been consistently keeping an eye on me and long ago had made the incorrect assumption that I was Jamaican, probably affiliated with a hard core Jamaican crew. For years, they were unable to pin down my true identity. All in all, my "island" cover created a smokescreen thick enough to shield me from close scrutiny, and was one of my most successful bluffs.

In due course, my adopted persona rubbed off on me. Rasta religion and culture became evermore fascinating, and in my early twenties, as a symbol of personal and spiritual evolution, I had the Lion of Judah tattooed on my left arm.

But in my early teens, I still had a long way to go on that evolutionary road.

Sticking, Reaching, Boosting

On a good day, picking pockets could add an additional three to four thousand bucks to our takings. We'd target a crowded thoroughfare, and one of us would *stick*, that is create the diversion to slow down foot traffic, while the other *reached*, slickly unloading the pockets and purses of our distracted victims.

We particularly liked working the big game venues: just a couple of cheeky kids weaving their way through the crowds, harmlessly enjoying the fun. There was a killing to be made at any event that involved crowds and confusion, and we'd always try and work the Rose Bowl, the Pro Bowl, the Orange Bowl, and the other *majors*, no matter how far we had to travel.

Boosting and fencing—stealing and "redistributing" other people's property—was also a tremendous revenue generator. We'd mobilize teams of kids and young women with instructions to "steal-to-order."

They'd hit busy shopping districts and malls, armed with lists of preordered items, and lift them off shelves and racks by the armload. Customer requests might be specific: a set of the red and white striped towels from Bloomingdales or a particular blue dress from Sears, size eight, please. And that's what we'd deliver.

There were hundreds of successful scams, but a few tried-and-tested favorites worked over and over. A young woman, for instance, would stuff a pillow up her dress, lock it in place with a girdle, pop her toddler into a pushchair, and rush into the targeted store appearing to be just another harried, young mother. Faster than whiplash, she'd swap the pillow—which got wedged into the pushchair—for ten pairs of jeans, three wadded-up shirts, a couple of summer dresses, and five sets of lingerie!

Layering worked pretty damn well, too. The *booster* would go into the changing room, carrying an armload of clothes to try on for size. She'd emerge, minutes later, fifty pounds heavier and many inches wider, and would simply walk, or more accurately waddle, right out of the store.

When plastic security tagging became popular, we had to get smarter, but a flathead screwdriver soon put paid to any problem with tags. Massive volumes of clothing, perfume, linens, jewelry, and make-up continued to flow past silent cash registers, out of store doors across Chicagoland.

What started as a small operation—a select team of "shoppers" hitting a few targeted stores—became a tightly coordinated, high-volume, high-margin business, and a major cash cow for us.

Thrill of the Game

By the late seventies, our various ventures were generating mountains of good, green paper. But, no matter how much poured in, I was perpetually on the hunt for more and *relentless* in my pursuit of profit. My mind hopped, like a flea in a jar, from one plan to the next, never still for a second, searching for the next scam.

> *If Burrel bought a house with three floors, he'd be trying to live on the fourth floor the next day—and when he saw there wasn't one, he'd go build it.*
> —Marcel Wilks

It perplexes me even today. What on earth drove me? Why did I continuously put myself in harm's way and risk everything for a few *quickpicks* here and there, that at best would only net me a few more bucks to add to the bankroll I already had?

To me, money was an *essential*, but largely *abstract* entity. Remember, I'd been raised at the knee of a drug kingpin. I was counting and stacking millions of dollars every week by the age of six. I knew money meant *power,* but I had absolutely no sense of its *value.* It was simply a commodity, a currency that you exchanged for something you considered to be of equal or greater value. No matter how much of the stuff you had, it could never, *ever* be too much.

Another motivation possibly lay in the seeds of misgiving germinating within me. I knew in my heart, that the flood of cash gushing into our pockets was a temporary phenomenon. It was essential to grab every cent of *today money,* I knew, because tomorrow the tap may be turned off. At thirteen years of age, I'd already seen too many squandered fortunes and ruined lives to have any belief that tomorrow was promised.

All of us kids lived in the moment and tried to wring as much life out of it as we could, but I'd been raised, in my father's image, to be a serious *playa.* And that's *exactly* what I was. For me, it was the sheer, heart-pounding, blood-singing, brain-stimulating *thrill* of the game that tugged me out of bed each day, ready to squeeze every ounce out of juice from my waking hours. To my mind, sleeping was just one step away from dying. Sometimes I'd run for up to three days and nights, without break, fuelled only by a diet of uppers, downers, and pure adrenaline.

A Corporate Kinda Guy

I formulated my own rules for how the game should be played, an area where Wenny and I diverged sharply, in philosophy and practice. I understood the benefits gained by bringing people together. I was a mediator and collaborator. Wenny, by contrast, was manipulative and divisive.

Self-preservation was a priority for all of us, but Wenny took it to a whole new level, turning it into an art form. He looked out only for number one—himself—a degree of self-immersion that prevented him from ever seeing the bigger picture.

Although a master of camouflage, I was *hopeless* at artifice. In my book, honesty and loyalty were the most precious of all human qualities. I never forgot those who stood by me. Wenny, on the other hand, would have sold his mother, if it gave him a chip in the game. Still, I knew the relationship he and I had could withstand any loyalty test. After a few years of experimenting with dirty tricks—most learned from Wiz—I concluded, with certainty, that the only way to play, and win, in the deadly game we were engaged in, was to play it *faster* and *better* than anyone else.

My mantra was to "always play fair," and I became known, even in the dubious and dangerous circles I moved in, as a man to be trusted, a man of his word. Wenny had no time for such principles. He was too busy scrambling up the ladder, without a thought for the breakages, betrayals, and bitterness left in his wake.

Unwittingly, my leadership style emulated that of some of the most successful managers in the corporate world. I built a tight, well-organized team with an "executive steering" committee and empowered "managers."[11] I mobilized, motivated, disciplined, and rewarded based on clearly defined codes of behavior. I played straight and tough, but fair,

---

11. See footnote 5, page 35, and for additional specifics on gang organizational structures, read Levitt and Dubner, *Freakonomics.*

and like all the best managers, I *grew* as I went along. I kept my eyes and mind open. Although I could talk up a storm, I also knew when to listen and learn.

I understood, at a deep level, that the real root of power lay not in ego-soaked individualism but in the ability to bring together multiple, self-interested groups, and choreograph their dance. I would be the button pusher I'd always aspired to be, the *king-maker,* and ultimately, the king.

Still Dancing

There was only one king of Cortez though. My father, indisputably, was master in our house. Wenny and I continued to break into his safe regularly in order to relieve him of some profit—not because we *needed* his money but because we could (it was not too difficult as I had the lock combination). Over the last five years, it had become a habit; yet another addiction we couldn't kick.

I suspect, without being able to articulate it at the time, I kept going back to drink from this particular well, as a way of getting back at my old man. As long as I was under his roof, I danced to his tune. He made sure I learned that lesson fresh every day. Whenever he felt like it, he'd jerk the leash a little tighter. I continued to carry the bulk of responsibility for the grocery store and was run ragged with whatever additional chores took his fancy that day. Thrashings were frequent, as were tears.

There's no question that my old man thrived on control. He controlled everyone around him and played all kinds of mental games. Using a potent combination of manipulation, retribution, and reward, he made certain his authority was unchallenged. He often threw Wenny in my face, jibing that I'd only made it as far as I had because of *his,* my dad's, clout; unlike Wenny, who'd achieved everything, flying solo.

That Dad seemed blind to Wenny's treachery and scheming and rated him so highly, often at my expense, puzzled me deeply and rankled for years. In the end, I guess it was just another of those choices we all make. Dad *chose* to see what he wanted to see, when it came to Wenny, who positively *radiated* charm in his presence. Wiz knew just what buttons to press.

Getting caught for the sin of stealing from my dad's safe was horribly inevitable, but I hadn't anticipated the way it would finally go down.

One day, when I was around thirteen, Burrel Senior discovered his money box missing from the safe. The box had contained about $120,000 in cash, and Dad never doubted for a second who was to blame. All roads led to me. It transpired that for years he'd known I regularly pilfered a few thousand from his take, yet he'd chosen to let it go. This time it was different though. Such a serious and direct challenge couldn't be ignored.

The theft of his cash box, an act so patently insulting it was tantamount to spitting in his eye, was a sign that I'd apparently lost all respect for his leadership. That night, when he burst into the basement apartment, he was *incandescent* with fury. As he hauled me out of bed, my stomach churned like a cement mixer. Flinching in anticipation of what was to come, I knew this was going to hurt, *bad*.

At the time, I had a shoulder-length *natural* that I'd proudly cultivated for years. You weren't a player if you didn't sport a *butter* and mine was one of the finest on the West Side. After beating the crap out of me with the knotted dog leash, Dad hauled me into the toilet and hacked all my hair off.

He held me, squirming and sniveling, by the scruff of my neck, with fingers of steel, as he chopped away. Through clenched teeth, he told me that we had a problem (I'd already figured *that* one out!), that he'd allowed me to be a grown man too soon, and as I couldn't *handle it*, he was *cutting* me down to boy-size again.

I'll *never, ever* forget that day. It was a scorcher, maybe around 85 degrees, the air liquid with humidity. I was wearing a black sock cap on my shorn head, to cover my humiliation, and was sopping wet, dripping with perspiration. My nose was broken, and I was bruised all over, but the old man kept heaping it on. He had me running to the store and any place else he could think of, to maximize my shame. No, I'll never forget that day. I was crying like a baby, naked and diminished like Samson without his hair, and hurting all over, inside and out.

Like other watershed moments in my life, I didn't realize the significance of this one until much later. Sure, I got kicked a little further down the road to adulthood, and lost my fine aquiline profile forever, but I inadvertently emerged with the mark of a leader stamped all over my head. Everyone who was *anyone* in the 'hood had long, natural hair—except me. I was a *man apart*.

And, of course, I hadn't stolen the cash box at all.

I'm certain to this day, the thief was Wenny, reinforcing my reluctant awareness that I couldn't trust that *son of a bitch* and shouldn't turn my back on him for a second. I knew I needed to sharpen my act, and fast.

CHAPTER SEVEN

Hundred Dollar Habits

1980–1983 (Age 13–15 Years)

Diversification and Commercialization

BETWEEN 1980 AND 1983, BUSINESS *EXPLODED,* and the burden of daily management became increasingly onerous. I didn't even go through the motions of pretending to attend school these days. All my free time was spent keeping the wheels of commerce turning. Our extended crew, including all runners and part-timers, now numbered several thousand, and we were positioning ourselves to be among the most powerful forces on the West Side.

We had more than twenty-one spots and ten smoke houses in our system. Four of the latter were combined with highly profitable gambling dens. We also had six stand-alone gambling houses. Our recent entry into organized gaming was paying off, royally.

Gambling was also the primary personal extravagance in which both Wenny and I indulged. Any cash we generated that wasn't immediately salted away usually went on one bet or another. We played craps, blackjack, and poker, and it wasn't unusual for $300,000 to change hands in a single throw of the dice. Playing only with each other at first, we soon realized the tremendous business opportunities offered by this recreational pursuit.

The Outfit, of course, had understood this for decades. Post-prohibition, gaming was seen as "the new booze." Even so, it wasn't until the early forties, after Sam Giancana had spent some cell time with an African-American gaming kingpin named Eddie Jones, that the Outfit's attention turned to the hitherto neglected area of "numbers." Prior to that, numbers, also known as the lottery, or policy, and a mainstay of the illicit ghetto economy, had been dismissed as "nigger pool" and was largely ignored by organized crime.[12]

In its heyday, the Outfit, under Tony Accardo, took a huge slice of the city's illicit gambling revenue, supplementing it with highly profitable loansharking. Times had changed though. With the legalization of gambling, the development of accessible casinos, and the advent of the national lottery, the pickings were thinner and the Outfit's interest had shifted in other directions.

Ours, on the other hand, was sharply focused on the possibilities presented by illegal gaming. Numbers were still popular on the West Side, but craps had become the premier game of chance in the ghetto. In craps, two dice are thrown in the hopes of getting a 7 or 11. The house wins on rolls of 2, 3, and 12. Lightning-fast, the game is particularly addictive because it is quick, easy, and immediate. Gamblers thrive off the head-rush they get from the moment, and tossing dice delivered an instant, *intense* high. In just a few seconds, a guy would know if it was *payday* or *pawn-day*. Thrown in alleys, on corners, and at the curbside, dice provided recreation and escapism, and injected a welcome element of chance into often dismal lives, turning dreams into *possibilities*.

It was a risky business though. Street-corner gamblers were always in danger of being shaken down themselves. A bunch of gang-bangers driving by, spotting a game in progress, knew immediately that there were easy pickings to be had. They'd hit hard, scoop up the pot, and probably break a few heads while they were at it.

Our dens offered a safe alternative to the street; a haven for the small

---

12. Gus Russo's *The Outfit* (Bloomsbury, 2003) paints a comprehensive picture of Outfit gambling and business interests. John Binder's, *The Chicago Outfit* (Arcadia Publishing, 2004) briefly, but succinctly, describes major shifts in Outfit operating strategy, from inception to the new millennium.

guys with *twos and fews* as well as high-rollers with suitcases of cash. The number of our gambling locations grew rapidly. They became great profit generators as well as convenient channels through which to launder money from other sources and change small bills into larger denominations.

A range of gaming options were on the menu but the consistent favorite was the craps table. *We* couldn't lose, whatever happened. The house would take a cut of all winnings—usually about 20 percent—but still we decided to weight the odds further in our favor. It was Wiz who suggested that the only smart gambler was a crooked one and that we should "fix" one of the tables. Always a guy with an eye for the main chance, I agreed readily enough.

We knew a guy who manufactured very clever dice tables. Both table and die were magnetized. Don't ask me to explain the science, but a magnetic field either attracts or repels another based on the positive or negative force of each. With the press of a button, the force of the table could be adjusted. In short, we could *gimmick* the die to fall whichever way the house needed them to.

Controls were cleverly integrated into a large silver belt buckle. I became highly adept at pressing the right buttons, using only sense of touch. I usually had custody of the belt while Wiz moved the game along. Being careful not to overplay our hand, we'd rotate the renegade tabletop between locations, but if through-traffic was good, the games lively, and the takings healthy, we'd put it to bed for the night. No point in spoiling a good thing.

For a street gambler, there's little to beat the excitement of determining your fortunes on a dice roll. Fuelled by testosterone and machismo, the size of some bets could make your eyes water! We ran games where the entry level was three million bucks, and I've seen the fate of up to twenty million, crisp, green ones decided on a single throw.

The most gut-wrenching loss I personally experienced was a $10 million betting disaster, when I was seventeen. In the space of no more than a few, *deeply* regrettable, seconds, I lost more money that most people could even hallucinate. Here's how it unfolded.

I showed up at the crap house on Quincy. Seven men were already there, in the throes of a major play. These guys were heavyweights. Big

Red was there, as well as Hineath, an Undertaker chief; Wenny; and a guy named Willy Cage, a topflight pimp. They were all kingpins, sitting on ridiculous cash surpluses. They played, as did I, solely with C-notes, and by the time I joined their little party, the spoils were stacked high.

The pot was brewing, $30 million strong, and Hineath was the key beneficiary. He was *sizzling,* and cocky, too. Not surprising considering he was sitting on winnings of about 19 million bucks. The other guys, badly burnt, were pulling back, but Hineath was hyped. The moment I walked in the door he was on me like white on rice.

"*Burrel!* Good to see you, bro! Now this here's a *real playa,* y'all, not like you coward *muthafuckers!* Let's roll dice, Burrel. What you shoot fo', man?"

"I ain't gambling tonight, Hi," I said. "I'm here pickin' up, not puttin' down."

"*Shiiiiit,* you gotta be kiddin'! All this money in the game, and you ain't *playin'?* Whassup, Burrel? You 'fraid to have money, man? What, you *scared* to have paper, King? If you scared to have money, then *here,* hold some of mine. Now you can play, bro." He waved wads of notes under my nose as he spoke.

These days I was sitting on my cash reserves, investing in property and projects, gambling only when the mood took me and when I felt the occasion was ripe. But like a dumb, hot-headed street kid, I let Hineath goad me into this high-rolling game. Usually I was the one in control, but I let him press my buttons and maneuver me into a place I knew I didn't want to go. Testosterone kicked in, and through a red mist, I became aware that I'd just committed to a $10 million wager. I swallowed hard.

Hineath tossed me a dice. "The biggest number goes first, King."

I rolled a three; he rolled a five.

"Ten million I shoot," he said, "five I hit."

I laid my stakes down. "No, I just got you on the fade, not the pass." He rolled. The dice hit the wall, clattering onto wood with a *rat-a-tat-tat* report that sounded louder to me than gunfire and, for a moment, drowned out the thud of my heart. It was nothing but a two-second roll, and in the deafening silence that followed, I knew, with the force of a sucker punch, that Hineath had beat me out of *10 million* big ones. He'd rolled an eleven.

The air quivered with tension, and Hineath, flushed and sweating with excitement, said again, "Ten I shoot, five I hit."

This time around, at a point when many gamblers make the fateful decision to chase their losses, a choice that invariably plummets them deeper into the abyss, the torrent of sanity that doused me was ice cold, shocking, and distinctly sobering.

"No way, man," I said. "I'm out. Yeah, right out. *For good.*"

From that day on, I never again gambled on a serious level.

Stress Fractures

Hairline cracks were appearing on the business front. Wiz and I were still tight personally and, along with Terence, drove operations, but the divide in our business philosophies and styles was yawning—and apparently, unbridgeable. Tensions escalated, and relationships were strained.

Despite growing dissent, we each were savvy enough to understand that a unified front was vital for survival. If we were to protect the whole shaky edifice we'd built, the turf we'd built it on, and our *lives*, then we had to work as one. Every day there were rebellions to quell, competitors to face off, and a hundred egos to juggle. And every second of every day, we were watching our backs, knowing that if a challenge were to come, it would likely be from someone we knew well. *No one* could be trusted.

Terence was and always would be a thug. He was a big guy and an accomplished fighter, probably the best within a range of at least six blocks. He was a classic "jailhouse boxer," the kind of guy who could beat his own shadow but didn't balk at a dirty trick or two. He might even have made it as a pro if he'd put his mind to it. But brutality was part of his DNA. Violence was his first, last, and only remedy for all situations, and he demonstrated little restraint, seeming to enjoy the act of meting out punishment.

At the slightest sign of dissent, egged on by Wenny, Terence would be mouthing off about *punkin'* this or that guy. That was Wiz's style all the way though: complicit but pretending not to be. He could set Terence off like a pit bull in a dogfight, and then completely disassociate himself from the consequences.

The preferred street-method of combat was known as *slap boxing*. A fast, deft sport, it called for nimble feet, a sharp eye, and quick hands, all resources I had in spades. I was more than a little handy. Apart from years of combat boot camp, courtesy of Dad, I'd studied kung-fu for more than three years, earning my black belt. But even though I could kick ass with the best, I did everything in my power to avoid violence.

Words and force of personality were *my* weapons of choice, my bullets. And highly effective they were, too. I was the mouth, the *Muhammad Ali*, of Cicero: mediating, cajoling, haranguing, persuading, and threatening. I rarely came up for air once on a roll. With my verbal armory fully deployed, a man might feel as though he were in front of a firing squad! Capitulation was common.

But things were heating up on the streets. The dynamics were changing. By the early eighties, the volume of narcotics flowing into the ghetto had transformed the face of black organized crime. *Hundreds of millions* of dollars were in play weekly. The price of merchandise continued to plummet, and the market grew exponentially. Gang-bangers were more heavily armed and more aggressive than ever; the ante was as high as it had ever been. Competition was deadly. Literally.

It was no longer a case of scrapping, slapping, and maybe stabbing a way through the turf wars with fists, boots, and knives. The gangs now relied on guns as their enforcers. Retribution could be grisly and permanent, but no matter how lethal, it never served to dampen the violence. One death would escalate to two or three or a dozen, as family, friend, and opportunist retaliated. Conflict spread like wildfires in a drought-dry forest.

Nobody ever said: "*Well damn*! He just killed Jimmy. *Fuck this bullshit;* let's stop the violence now!"

No, it was far more likely that before nightfall, Jimmy would be avenged in blood, and another young black man added to the body count.

I knew the situation was only going to get hotter, and *no one* could possibly win. Homicide had no part in my world. Only a fool goes with violence as a strategy; it takes a stronger man to use words. The only possible winners of a shoot-out were the undertakers and lawyers. As one mother buries her son, another is preparing herself, emotionally, for decades of prison visits. She, at least, will see her boy again, and not have to settle for kissing and weeping over his picture on a tombstone.

I faced my own mortality up close and personal at fifteen, when I inadvertently became embroiled in a turf battle that was a hair's breadth from an all-out, full-fledged war. I looked death in the eye and said *no!*

We'd been operating a spot—one that was making about $50,000 to $60,000 a day—on Laverne, opposite a similar corner operated by the Dangars, a couple of brothers running under the emblem of the Souls. Raking in even more than we did each day, they got greedy and began to eye our patch. While smiling to our faces, they connived behind our backs and, in due course, hired a stickup guy to close us down.

He hit our spot and robbed it. After much debate, argument—and restraining of Terence—we "turned" the same stickup guy, sending him back across the road to return the favor. Things escalated rapidly, getting nasty, fast. Word soon reached us that the Dangars had mobilized a street force of more than 150 guys to move against us.

A killing seemed inevitable, and I knew there was a bullet with my name on it. As a CIVL chief, I'd be one of the first in the cross-hairs. The tension of not knowing from where and when the hit would come was excruciating. It was time to leverage my power. I contacted Codeine, another CIVL chief, who in turn called Sam McKay, the formidable leader of the Souls.[13]

Sam and I had hung out for years, but I learned early on never to take anything for granted on the streets. He had to look at the *big* picture, and I made sure I always treated our relationship with due respect. A meeting between Sam, the Dangar brothers, and me was arranged for the next day. We met in Le Clair Park, where Sam liked to play chess.

Without raising his eyes or voice, Sam controlled the meeting from the get-go:

"You got anything against Burrel, bro?" he addressed Maurice, the older of the Dangars.

"No." Begrudgingly.

Sam was silent.

Maurice again. "No, man. We ain't got no beef."

---

13. Having been convicted of murder, Sam McKay is currently serving a sixty-five- year sentence in the penitentiary.

Sam looked up now. "Burrel? That cool wit' you, man?"

"Yeah, Sam. Cool."

"Good." Sam went back to the chessboard without another word.

Just like that, it was over. That's how simple it can be when three giants get together and use words—no matter how few—rather than guns.

But the alarm bells jangling in the back of my mind wouldn't be silenced. I knew this reprieve from a potentially fatal confrontation was temporary. The next challenge wouldn't come from the Dangars. It might come from a rival faction fighting for turf, or from some ambitious young VL buck intent on climbing the power ladder—some youngsters coming through the lines displayed levels of callousness that shocked even the OGs—or the threat was just as likely to come from someone I trusted. He might be one of my own crew, thirsty and impatient for rank. Or he might be a good friend.

I knew, before too long, I'd be forced to make a stand. It seemed inevitable that I'd either have to take a life or lose mine. Neither alternative was acceptable.

My only other option was to break away completely. That thought took root on fertile ground and began to sprout like one of those garden weeds my dad could never get rid of.

I was becoming increasingly disillusioned with my crew. Wenny's betrayals and Terence's brutishness were amplified by innumerable instances of cheating and thievery among guys I should have been able to trust with my back. The stakes were higher than ever, but few of my *rappits* (crew) were stepping up. Leery and mistrustful to the point of paranoia, I was on edge constantly. This state of mental and physical exhaustion was exacerbated by the chemically fuelled marathons that kept me up for days on end.

I was running on fumes.

Money Before Sense

On the operational front, Wiz and I may have diverged sharply, but as far as spending money was concerned, we were two sides of the same coin. The vast amount of cash pouring in had long since outstripped our ability to effectively clean and consume it, so we hid the stuff in a wide variety of nooks, crannies, and corners around the neighborhood; some subtle, others not.

Scratch was wedged under floors and piled up in empty apartments. It was jammed into mailboxes and wardrobes; stuffed behind pipes, under mattresses, and into ventilation shafts. It filled attics and the spare wheel compartments of a number of cars parked in various odd places, and it spilled out of black plastic sacks in basements.

We carried bags of it with us, too. I always carried enough paper to choke a horse, at least $10,000 in cash. Wenny did the same. I'd bought a square, brown briefcase especially for the job. I must have made a incongruous sight: a flashy black kid in his tailored suit, packing a gun and dripping in diamonds, lugging around such an emblem of corporate conservatism. I've never doubted though, that across the world, there are armies of equally unlikely folk carrying innocuous, brown briefcases stuffed to the brim with illicit cash.

Of all the dumb things I've done in my life, one of the dumbest *ever,* was to burn money, I mean literally *watch it go up in smoke!*

On Friday nights, our little crew often gathered together, huddling in the warmth and privacy of the small garage at the back of the house in Cortez Street. Lighting a fire in the old barbeque pit in the garden, we'd char-grill steaks and, when we were done eating, would hold dollar bills against the burning embers and watch as they flared briefly and then, slowly and blackly, crackled and curled into dust.

Ignorant, brash kids, busy trying to impress each other—and anyone else who happened to be around—we thought we were *big shots*. I got the idea of burning cash from some Greek buddies. For them, it was a symbolic gesture, usually reserved for times of celebration. We, of course, took it to a whole new level of *idiocy* as we tried to out-cool each other. Burning our way through several thousand dollars a session, we nonchalantly watched fortunes go up in smoke.

And don't think the only way to burn money is with fire. I had *dozens* of other strategies that worked just as well, each and every one of which would be put into practice over the next ten years.

Oh, yes, I definitely got my money *before* I got my sense.

The Finer Things

Wenny and I shared a love of fine clothes and jewelry, sharp shoes, girls, Cristal champagne, and cars.

While Wiz spent a fortune on tailored clothes, he was quirky when it came to shoes, being more of a never-mind-the-quality-feel-the-width kind of guy. If he had to make a choice between ten pairs of imitation-crocodile shoes, or one sharp pair of Gucci loafers for a thousand bucks, he'd grab the crocs *right away*. The end result was an odd mix of couture, ghetto-chic, and flash-trash.

Our minds converged on the subject of cars though. We acquired our first car as a joint investment, when I was eight and Wenny eleven. It was a black-and-white top '69 Plymouth, fondly known as "The Punkmobile." For a few months, that car became our trusted runaround—even though I had to sit almost vertically, propped up on a pile of books, for my feet to reach the pedals. Eventually, we moved up the automotive ladder and graduated to proud ownership of the infamous "Cadi-Club-Coupe," Trey's turbo-charged Buick!

The first car I owned exclusively was a beautiful bronze Cadillac. I was thirteen years old and had always wanted one. Cadillacs were big in my neighborhood. My dad drove one, as did many of our relatives. I have fond memories of great *Cadi-convoys* heading down south on road trips. A car with attitude and enough flash for even the most flamboyant pimp, the Cadi was a popular ghetto status symbol. Being more than familiar with this sweet ride, I slipped behind the wheel like *water on wax*. That first Cadillac was followed by a long parade of beauties, but I didn't get my first Rolls Royce until I came of age at sixteen.

Wenny and I started a major new trend in car ownership. The police, it appeared, never singled out crappy, worn-out cars for a stop-and-search. We decided to get smarter and use what we called *traps* for day-to-day business matters. We built up a fleet of tired old jalopies, rescued from scrap heaps outside the neighborhood, squeezing out whatever little life was left in them. But when the day was done and we were dressed to party, we would haul out the brand new, sleek thoroughbreds: Benzes for me and Volvos for Wenny.

Over the years, Wiz and I each became strongly associated with these brands. My stable of vehicles always featured at least two or three

Mercedes—usually silver—and Wenny usually bought the latest model of Volvo as soon as it hit the showrooms. Not exactly streamlined, fleet-footed beasts, Volvos were smooth, solid, and reliable. I know Wenny always felt safe when tucked behind the wheel of this benignly disguised "armored" car.

It was bitterly ironic, then, that he would lose his life in one.

Wine, Women, and Song

From the age of eight, I'd played around with girls. I lost my virginity at eleven, for a price, to an obliging second cousin. Burrel Senior encouraged my precociousness. He even experimented with pimping himself—though strictly small-time—and regularly socialized with other heavy-duty pimps.

It was no news to me then that sex and money went hand in hand. Mature beyond my years in many respects, in others I was still a kid. I didn't have the necessary years in my *experience* bank account to have developed fully on some key emotional dimensions. I'd simply been around *too few* years to have an evolved understanding of the emotional interplay around sex—its subtext—or when it came to that, to understand much about love at all.

To me the equation was simple: sex equaled dollars.

Sex was just like any other transaction involving merchandise: you paid for it, you consumed it, you felt good, and then you bought some more. It wasn't such a great stretch from here, to see sex as a mutually beneficial commercial exchange, a belief that colored my attitude for many years.

Wiz and I bought expensive suits by the dozen and Cristal by the case. We threw wild parties and lavished money on our cars, but everything else in which we indulged was pretty much free. Our supplies of drugs and women were virtually unlimited, and anything else we needed—or desired—such as jewelry or fine linens could be stolen to order.

By now, we had the *big-bill* habit bad! C-notes were our currency of choice, and we'd deal only in crisp, green hundred dollar bills. Much as we loved 'em, the challenge of exchanging mountains of small denominations for larger bills each week became a big headache, requiring us to find ever more creative ways to launder funds.

I always carried bundles of pristine notes on my person, and the thrill of flicking a new hundred out of my over-stuffed money clip, to tip a waiter or grease the palms of the doorman at a flashy steakhouse, never diminished.

R&R (Rhythm and Rollers)

I had enough cash to do, or buy, pretty much anything I wanted, but if you were to ask me what my real recreational passion was, I'd have to say it was the simple pleasure of *rhythm skating*. As a way of letting off steam, easing my overcrowded mind, and working off the excessive energy I'd been blessed with from birth, it couldn't be beaten.

From the age of ten, well into my twenties, whenever I could, I roller-skated. Physically taxing, skating demanded a different kind of concentration and usually proved to be the perfect antidote to the mounting demands of my pressure-cooker world.

Gang chief, business tycoon, and dutiful son by day—those evenings I spent at the rink, I was just a kid again. The "Concrete Jungle"—later known as "Hot-Wheels"—was a cavernous arena located on Pulaski and Chicago. In this deafening place, laughter and shrieks mingled with ear-splitting beats, pumping out of enormous speakers suspended from the ceiling. The place was a wall of sound, pulsating with *pure energy*.

Rhythm skating is exactly what it sounds like it should be: a group of kids get together and *dance* on roller-skates. We'd synchronize choreography and practice as a team, but there was plenty of room too for crowd-pleasing, ego-propelled solo performances. Fast, complicated, and risky routines were our specialty. Leaps, splits, wheelies, and intricate dance-steps guaranteed we were the main attraction whenever we showed up.

Dancing only to James Brown—JB—*man*, we'd fly! "Watergate" was my personal favorite, but *anything* by JB would get those wheels spinning. I proudly sported a pair of Jym2 skates, the Rolls Royce of the genre, with high boots, high stepper wheels, and Snyder plates.

Cool indeed, they were the envy of all the skating pros and great for pulling chicks!

Feeding the Dragon

Ah. If only skating had been my sole recreation. If only life could always be as uncomplicated as during those hours spent twirling, twisting, and leaping. But it wasn't. By now, I was a heavy drug user with a habit that became more voracious by the day.

I'd smoked pot for the first time, sanctioned by my dad, at age seven. By now, I was inhaling a minimum of an ounce and a half each day. More deadly than my marijuana habit, though, was my growing addiction to *cough syrup*. I'd drink *anything* I could get over, or under, the counter. After a few swigs of that pungent, viscous liquid, the world was rosy again. That wonderful glow would steal slowly through my stressed-out body and I would just curl up in its warmth. Soon I'd be blinking and nodding, cocooned in my own cozy drowsiness.

But, in reality, no one operating in my world could afford to close their eyes for more than a minute or two. So in order to offset this self-induced *soporific-ness*, I added cocaine to my narcotic cocktail. Always a man of extremes, when I snorted coke, I snorted *a lot* of it. By the time I was fourteen, I was getting through an ounce a day and then some. When heroin—that most addictive of poisons—became plentiful in the early eighties, that too was liberally mixed into the brew.

In the language of the world I inhabited, my drug habits didn't label me a junkie. In my 'hood you were only considered a junkie—and by extension, a sad, sorry loser—when you injected the stuff. As long as we just swallowed, smoked, or snorted our daily diet of narcotics, folks like me considered ourselves to be recreational users, not addicts.

But it was still a deadly concoction that rotted your teeth, destroyed your nasal passages, addled your brain, and melted your guts.

It would be another two years before I kicked my drug habit, and I don't exaggerate when I tell you, I went to some dark, desperate places. It's little short of a miracle that I survived these kamikaze years.

Forging My Own Path

Drug-sodden though I was, I was also brim-full with passion and ambition, and my sense of destiny remained unwavering. This was my *secret sauce*. I *knew*, with absolute certainty, that I had the ability to be anything

I wanted to be if I just put my mind to it. It's unlikely that in those days what I wanted to be would have impressed many. I aspired to be the most respected chief, the richest hustler, and the most powerful *playa* in the ghetto. These were the goals that got me out of bed every day and put fire in my belly.

At fifteen, I had all the power and wealth a man should have been able to handle. One of the funny things about life, though, is when you're a kid, you take risks you don't have to. I was still out there every day, running capers, *sweating* the *small* stuff.

It was important to me, to stay close to the front line. Most chiefs rely on their runners, but I always put myself squarely in the center of things. Even as a chief, I felt a strong compulsion to demonstrate to my crew how "it"—whatever "it" happened to be—should be done. I guess I inherited more than a few of my dad's controlling tendencies!

Daily immersion in the grimy stuff kept me firmly grounded though. Paradoxically, it probably kept me out of more trouble than it put me in. A lot of guys in the penitentiary are there, because they lost touch with the reality of the streets. Convinced they were far enough removed from the fire to escape the heat, they'd get complacent and drop their guard. I wasn't about to make the same mistake.

Heavily into camouflage, I covered my tracks well. Discretion and organization were necessary in order to set things up in a way that didn't look *set up*. I was a master at both. In the ghetto, everyone knows everyone else's business, and though secrets were valuable currency, my lips remained sealed. I kept confidences and didn't boast about my business interests, or the interests of others. I was recognized in leadership circles as a *quiet giant*.

My trump cards were my passion, energy, and individuality. I earned trust and respect through strength of character, consistent fair play, and sheer force of personality. Like my father, I was my *own man*, a natural leader. Respected by the streets, I refused to let them consume me.

Burrel was unique. You know, there are guys who need to run with a crowd. They draw their energy from it. Well, Burrel was different. It was like, he was electric, like he was his own energy source.

—Big C

Sometimes I covered my tracks too well. As a consequence, I could be underestimated. Stepping out of the long shadow cast by my dad was never going to be easy. He was *the man*. No one was getting down like my father. People respected the hell out of him but were sometimes ready to cross his son. "He's cool," they'd say, "but I really want to get up with his old man."

There were a lot of guys who *needed* to make excuses in their minds as to why I was so advanced. They explained it away by attributing my success to my dad's power, and the influence of the older guys I ran with—guys like Big John and Sam McKay. By giving me little personal credit, it helped them reconcile the reality of a young guy making millions with their own lagging fortunes.

Wenny was convinced I was reliant on him. He shared a common belief with my dad that I wouldn't be where I was today without him. Neither he nor Burrel Senior acknowledged my capacity for leadership and for years underrated my ability, drive, and determination. They viewed me as a follower and foot soldier, elevated only through family connections. I let them believe it. Like a chameleon, I found that masking my true ambitions and abilities gave me a significant edge.

Wiz had no lack of drive or application either, but his gasoline was mostly egotism and greed. His lack of scruples was increasingly unsettling. By now, there was little in the manner in which he operated that was reconcilable with my own code of behavior. As he gambled, got high, and played around, I continued to build my own more strategic operations.

CHAPTER EIGHT

Playing With The Big Boys

The Outfit

EVOLUTION HAS BEEN A HALLMARK OF THE OUTFIT SINCE ITS POST-PROHIBITION BIRTH. The Outfit, in short, is a criminal enterprise organized for the profit of its members. Opinion has it that the Outfit is probably the most successful of any group of organized criminals in the United States.

Part of La Cosa Nostra (LCN), a loose affiliation of major-city gangs cooperating nationally through a "commission," the Outfit parlayed its hold over local political and union organizations into control of regional and national entities. Ultimately, its influence extended *way* beyond the boundaries of Chicago, with tentacles reaching as far afield as Los Angeles, Vegas, and even Cuba.

Since its inception, the Outfit has been run by a consistently strong and surprisingly stable leadership, resulting in an unusually cohesive organization. Ruled for the most part by a single, powerful dynasty, there was far less dissent and infighting than, for example, in New York, where five "families" competed for dominance. Though not averse to some serious heavy-handedness, the Outfit's modus operandi was generally astute, strategic, and increasingly "corporate."

But Tony "Big Tuna" Accardo's recent visits to the West Side were indicative of changing times for the Mob. The world had moved on, and although still a force to be reckoned with, the Outfit was no longer the powerhouse organization it had been.[14]

Radical shifts in business interests, public attitude, and policing policy had diminished the family's union and government influence, as had the city's changing demographics. Although the Outfit was more diverse than most other families, the growth of Chicago's ethnic population and the subsequent swings in political alignments had eroded its power base substantially.

Many of the businesses upon which its post-Prohibition fortunes were built were now available *legally*. The state lottery and easy-access casinos bit deeply into gambling revenue, and more relaxed social mores had long since made the business of vice less financially attractive. No, the *big money* had moved into narcotics, and this was an arena in which the Outfit, under Accardo's leadership, *refused* to play.

Probably the greatest factor in the Outfit's financial decline, though, was the extreme pressure applied by the Feds—the Gs. From 1966 onwards, every Outfit leader, with the exception of Tony, had done prison time—and Tony came pretty damn close in the sixties, when he was convicted of tax evasion.[15]

The organization still held low-key interests in vice, chop-shops, gaming, and protection; and it continued to reach into other Midwest cities as well as Los Angeles and Vegas. But over the years, the Outfit had progressively moved its assets into *quasi-respectable* businesses such as transport, restaurants, and real estate.

So the Tony Accardo, who came to meet with the Vice Lords that day

---

14. John Binder's, *The Chicago Outfit* (Arcadia Publishing, 2004) briefly, but succinctly, describes major shifts in Outfit interests and operating strategies, from its post-Prohibition inception into to the new millennium.

15. Tony may have evaded a prison sentence, but the Feds continued to apply relentless pressure, and, as recently as April 2005, announced sweeping indictments against the Outfit. In that month, "Operation Family Secrets" netted a number of important Outfit leaders (although Joey Lombardo, the alleged head of the organization, managed to evade arrest). Prosecutors charged the entire Outfit as a criminal enterprise. Eighteen murders and one attempted murder were attributed to the Chicago mob as part of this action.

in 1978, favored a different negotiating style than the Tony "Joe Batters" Accardo who enforced his orders with the blunt end of a bat. Tony accepted the realities of the new face of Chicago organized crime, and was prepared to work with it—and with us.

He was everything that a boss should be. He stayed out of the media spotlight—something his successor Sam Giancana failed to do, and paid for with his life.[16] He was a man's man and a family man. Tony would never do anything to compromise his strong family values or bring disrepute on the Outfit. Even after he'd officially stepped down as boss in '57, he remained the power behind the throne. As the Outfit's "Chairman of the Board," he represented them nationally, on the LCN Committee, until the day he died in 1992.

Tony was like an old, turn-of-the-century Mafia don in Sicily. Formidable yet surprisingly magnanimous, he wielded his power evenly and without arrogance. *No one* challenged his authority. "Joe Batters" never had to look over *his* shoulder—the only people behind him were watching his back. If you crossed him though, you'd better start looking over *yours*.

But, of course, we *ghetto-niggas* were far too ignorant to grasp this! To us, guys like Tony were history. They represented the *old way,* and today, across the West Side and large chunks of the South Side, it was the day of the *black man.* Guys like Tony couldn't operate on our turf, and they sure couldn't follow us home if we decided to hit and run on theirs.

This was another of the ways in which we proudly cultivated our ghetto-mentality. The ghetto, without doubt, offered a secure base of operations. We could operate behind its fortress-like boundaries with impunity or retreat into the safety of its streets at will. But few of us had the foresight to understand that we were actually building our own prisons, locking ourselves in and *throwing away the key.*

---

16. Sam "Mooney" Giancana was deposed as mob front man in 1966, as he emerged from a year behind bars. His furious political feuding with the Kennedys; his lavish, high-profile Vegas lifestyle, in the company of Frank Sinatra; and his legal activity (he sued the FBI for harassment) had became intolerable to Accardo and Ricca. He moved to Mexico, thriving financially for years, until in 1974 when he was kicked out and deported without a dime. In 1975, he was shot dead in the basement of his Oak Brook apartment, after a favorite meal of sausages.

Walking and Talking

This then was the giant, this legend named Tony Accardo, who for some personal and largely unfathomable reason took me under his wing when I was just a kid. He loved River Forest with a passion, and we'd stroll for hours around the neighborhood, shooting the breeze.

He saw something in me, he said. He liked my style and my attitude. I had an *old soul,* he joked, and had clearly lived many previous lives on this earth. He also told me it was time for me to make some tough choices.

"Burrel, if I gave you the choice of being a big fish in a small pool in the ghetto," he said one day as we were circling the block on foot, "or a hungry minnow in a bigger pond . . ." he stopped walking and turned to me, "What answer would you give me?"

It took me less than a second to respond. "A big fish," I said. "In fact, the *biggest* fish. I'm going be *king* of the West Side!"

Tony looked at me thoughtfully and resumed walking slowly. After a moment or two, he turned to me again and shook his head. "Wrong answer, kid. Wrong answer."

It took me a while to understand what Tony was talking about, and during the many hours across the many years that we spent walking and talking, Tony did more than anyone to finally pry open my eyes and force me to see my life in a different light. But even as that light tentatively flickered on, I did everything within my power to turn it *off.* Self-awareness arrived slowly and painfully, my mind and internal survival mechanisms screaming *blue murder* at every glimmer that got through the blinds.

Insight is often unwelcome because with it comes responsibility. As the depressing consciousness of the ugliness, grubbiness, and *smallness* of my world seeped into me, it became tougher to ignore. I saw, starkly, the harm I was causing others and myself, and that I needed to find an alternative path. Reluctantly, I began to open my mind to the possibility that there was a bigger apple out there. I needed to take a bite of it. I just didn't know how.

When I look back on my relationship with Tony, I see that he took up where my dad left off. Here I was again, at the knee of a *giant.* My dad had started with a blank canvas on which to paint his image, but Tony took on the much tougher task of scraping off some of the old paint, and fashioning a fresh portrait.

So it was Tony "Big Tuna" Accardo who told me my clothes looked like *ghetto-trash*; that it was embarrassing to have me come to his home looking this way; that I needed to stop being a junkie and *sort myself out*; that there was a whole, wide world out there and, in the greater scheme of things, I was just a two-bit player.

What did Tony get out of this strange relationship? It's hard to say really, but I suspect he enjoyed my energy and, maybe surprisingly, my impertinence and irreverence. Consistently surrounded by the sycophantic and subservient, I think Tony found our verbal sparring refreshing and stimulating. I knew how to wind him up, and could *always* get him steaming under the collar.

A proud, hot–blooded Italian through and through, Tony liked to hang with me. And if there was something to be gained from it, he wasn't averse to working with other nationalities either, but he wasn't exactly an advocate of interracial relations. Let's be honest, Tony was a bigot, and most the guys he ran with were bigots, too. He'd crack on me all the time, about being an honorary Italian, albeit a black one but *hated* it when I turned the tables.

"Look at you, man! Look at your dark skin and hair, and them brown eyes. Man, your grandma must have messed around with a black man. You're just a white nigga!" I'd whoop, "*a wop nigga!*"

Tony would redden and give me The Look. "Burrel, you shut up with that talk. You keep saying that kind of shit, and you'll find yourself riding home in the car trunk."

But we had serious conversations, too. I walked around those blocks with Tony trying to extract his knowledge and absorb his experience. I wanted him to show me how I could become a real smooth player like him. But he would have none of it. No, Tony had a whole different agenda. In all the time I spent with him, even knowing my power and connections, he *never* tried to recruit me. Instead he prodded and pushed and badgered me to get out of the game. Tony used to tell me that he'd got caught up young, and, in his world, once you were in, there was no getting out. Maybe he even saw me as a second chance to extract himself, vicariously.

Whatever his motives, I used to fob him off with the same tired old line: "I'm gettin' out, Tony. I am; I'm really goin' to get out."

"Well, what's wrong with today, Burrel? Today is a good day. Today you don't have a problem. Tomorrow you might."

And that's what I kept hearing in my head. "*Today you don't have a problem; tomorrow you might.*" And I knew he was right. Today I didn't have a problem, but tomorrow I might just die.

Heady Times

A mentor rather than business partner, Tony generally kept me apart from the Outfit's business. Sure, we cooperated on the issue of keeping River Forest as secure as possible, and for some time after those initial meetings at Tony's home, a few of us succeeded in doing just that. Using power and position, we greased palms and kicked some butts, and for a few short months, peace reigned in the *home of the hoods*.

The street-pact was high-maintenance, though, and took tremendous amounts of time and energy. Inevitably, as loyalties and alignments shifted, and eroded, cooperation between different factions unraveled. Soon there were new encroachments across Austen. But by then, my relationship with Tony had moved on.

Although I never really got close to the workings of the Outfit, there were more than a few memorable occasions when I was invited to Tony's house to join informal gatherings. These meetings usually took place in the basement of the house on Ashland Terrace. In fact, the only time I saw any other floor was on camera, the day following Wenny's raid. I was even grateful to him for those indiscretions, because of which I knew even the bathroom was wired. That intelligence prevented me from doing some *very dumb* things, like sneaking off to inhale a line of coke, an act that would likely have ended my strange friendship with Tony somewhat prematurely.

The basement area of Tony's house had been especially designed for gatherings like these. Running down the center of the thickly carpeted room was a large oak table, oval in shape, with seating for twelve people. There was, of course, a wine cellar, a well-patronized wet bar— a prerequisite for male bonding—and a bowling alley, but no TV or pool table.

The walls were laden with evidence of Tony's commitment to his family.

Photographs depicting his wife and children, smiling and progressively maturing, were proudly displayed throughout. But the key reason this room was perfect for private meetings was that, like Vegas, what happened here, *stayed* here. There was no chance anyone could listen in—except me, of course, but then I'd been invited.

Sitting quietly on the periphery of the party, I listened with the same kind of thirstiness I'd had as a six-year-old, sitting at my dad's side, hanging onto his every word. Conversation swirled through the air as thickly as the clouds of cigarette and cigar smoke. Discussions ran from business and politics to family and relatives. The talk, though innocuous on the surface, proffered rich pickings for an astute listener with the mental agility to connect the dots. I soaked it up, inadvertently absorbing a great deal of intelligence relating to the commercialization of crime, politics, and business strategy.

I wonder what these guys made of me over those years: a young, flashy black kid, sometimes in the thick of things, but more often than not, sitting on the edges listening and watching quietly. Over time I became a familiar face.

Interestingly, Capone's Syndicate, the Outfit's predecessor, was possibly one of the least prejudiced crime organizations of its time. Capone made an enormous contribution to the Chicago jazz scene and to the careers of many black artists. Bringing them into the city, he'd give them a break at one of his entertainment joints, apparently paying well.

The Outfit, while not quite following in Capone's footsteps in this regard, was also known as relatively diverse culturally. They certainly did business with other blacks, but though I witnessed Caucasians of various exotic descent descend the stairs to Tony's basement meetings, I never saw another black face. I guess diversity only goes so far, and inviting it into your house is a whole different ball game.

It wasn't only the conversations that were heady at these get-togethers. I was intoxicated by the entire sensory experience. Sometimes I'd smoke, take a drink, or join the conversation, but truth be told, I was at my happiest when removed from the general hubbub. Easing myself apart, I'd take in the whole scene from what sometimes seemed like the far side of a two-way mirror.

Interpreting the complex interpersonal dynamics in that room was one of my favorite pastimes: eager expressions and surly countenances; flat, facial inscrutability betrayed by hands that gave it all away; bodies leaning in and eyes darting out.

I let myself roll with the ebb and flow of male conversation, punctuated by surges of laughter and voices raised in emphasis. The clink of glasses and the throaty *glug-glug-glug* of decanting whiskey and wine added a subtle percussion to this gentle cacophony, its sharp edges muffled by smoke and thick carpet. Oh, yes, a man could get high on this.

Old Blue Eyes

Faces flowed through the house on Ashland Avenue. Confident, arrogant, obsequious, enigmatic, sometimes angry, and sometimes scared, they came and went. The Outfit's main players, men with the collective ability to wield and manipulate power and wealth on an almost inconceivable level, all passed through that subterranean meeting room at some point.

Rough elements mingled with the debonair. Big, bluff, and swarthy men joined furtive, smoky, and seedy characters who blended with the cool, confident, and brash. By and large, though, Tony's visitors were men of substance and not a little style, immaculately clad in the finest examples of Italian tailoring in silk and cashmere.

On two occasions, my world shifted on its axis due to the charismatic pull of one of Tony's guests. These were the days Frank Sinatra breezed into the basement. I thought I had died and gone to heaven.

Frank joined a couple of social sessions at Tony's house as a guest, and our meetings, though brief, were *glitteringly* memorable. Handsome and charming, he *exuded* cool from every lived-in pore. I was introduced, and we exchanged a few comments about his health, his music, and my admiration. He sang a couple of songs at Tony's behest. "That's Life" will forever be my favorite Sinatra melody. This song is my anthem, its lyrics my storyline.

The personal impact of meeting this legend was incalculable. I sucked up his music as greedily as I used to suck up syrup. Soon I was word-perfect in an entire repertoire of Sinatra songs. His style and sassiness blew me away. From the moment we met, the impression of Frank insisted on tiptoeing into my world. I became an ardent Rat Packer wannabe.

For a long time, Los Angeles had been tucked in the back of my mind as a place I needed to see; now I added Vegas to my mental list of new frontiers.

Vegas

Wenny and I made our first trip to Vegas when I was fourteen. My desire to visit this Bugsy Siegel creation, this desert city of casinos and bright lights, had new urgency since my historic meeting (well, *historic* as far as I was concerned) with Frank Sinatra, so Wiz and I set off for Vegas with great anticipation.

Vegas didn't disappoint. We gambled our way around the place, observing the mechanisms of the business of gaming. We flashed our credentials, made some important connections, lost money, drank too much, and soaked it all up. It was in Vegas that we got the idea to "fix" our own games.

But in time, cards, dice, roulette wheels, dancing girls, and glitzy shows were all displaced by the delights of boxing! Nothing could beat the thrill of VIP seats at a hot fight at Caesar's Palace, and a high-stakes bet on the outcome. Dropping $50,000 or more a fight wasn't an unusual occurrence for us.

Wiz and I heeded the siren call of Vegas dozens of times over the next six years or so—and I continued to visit long after he and I had parted company. In all those trips, the high point for me was front row seats at the Sugar Ray Leonard vs. Tommy "Hit-Man" Hearns fight in '81. Sugar Ray whomped his ass![17]

Other Voices

Inner conflict—as I straddled the two worlds of the 'hood and Tony's realm—was chewing me up by the time I hit my mid-teens. My lifestyle was increasingly at odds with the emotions swirling around inside me.

---

17. Boxing in the late seventies and early eighties was a compelling sport, populated with colorful characters and real superstars such as George Foreman, Sugar Ray Leonard, Michael Spinks, and Larry Holmes. The sport today, as it potentially moves toward a greater degree of federal regulation, is lackluster in comparison.

Layers of ghetto conditioning and a diamond-hard shell of self-interest had insulated me from "too much" self-awareness for most of my life. But my protective shield was crumbling.

Doubt squirreled its way into my brain, and the voices of my guides, mentors, heroes, and conscience became an ear-splitting, internal chorus. I had to shut them up, dull them down, or drown them out, and the only way to do that was with more pills, more scams, and a steady diet of cocaine.

But they weren't going to go quietly.

At fifteen, I was already a father of two, having conceived two sons a year earlier. I didn't handle fatherhood well. My relationships with the boys' mothers were volatile at best. In reality, I was an irresponsible kid who, though entering parenthood with his eyes open, had no concept of what being a father really meant. I was still a boy myself, and a selfish one at that. Wrestling with my own demons, I was riddled with drug addiction and preoccupied with trying to figure out what my next moves would be. I had neither the emotional bandwidth—nor the will—to take on a dependent.

My first son was lost to me early on when his mother's family adopted him and moved from Chicago. My second son, Marshawn, also moved in with his mom's family, and as I drifted further from her, I drifted far from him, too. Marshawn would come back into my life much later, and his loss, the second time around, would be much harder to bear.

Chemical Engineering

I continued to get high, and low, and high again, whenever I could. Ironically, by transporting me into my own private world, my diet of uppers and downers enabled me to carve out slices of space for meditation and introspection. Such moments were often accompanied by unwelcome clarity.

I used this headroom for some straight talking. I told myself that soon I was going to give all this up; that I'd buy one respectable business or another, and stop hanging out on street corners, taking stupid risks and doing wrong. Uncompromisingly tough, I berated myself endlessly for the damage I was causing to myself and others and for still being in the game, when I knew I should long since have left it behind.

So, somewhat paradoxically, taking drugs created oases of calm in the midst of my crazy, frenetic, jittery, paranoid world, and I used those *quiet* times to talk myself *out* of taking drugs. I felt like I was watching my own struggle on TV, a young foolish guy scrabbling for sense.

Slowly but surely, I was making headway. As I pried my mind open, a millimeter at a time, glimmers of light were shining through the cracks.

Using determination and willpower, I began cutting back on the drugs I used. I wanted to go *cold turkey*, but just couldn't do it right off. Every time I'd try, I'd struggle through two or three weeks before finding some excuse, or some reason, to celebrate or commiserate. I'd be off the wagon and back on the stuff in a moment. Rationalizing that I couldn't go to anyone else for help—they hadn't told me to *start* so they sure couldn't tell me to *stop*—I shouldered the load myself. If I was to escape addiction, I knew the strength had to come from *inside*. My body and my mind would tell me when it was ready, and I conditioned myself in preparation for that moment.

But I had a long way to go before I'd kick the habit. I refined the *science* of engineering my days and nights chemically, for optimum efficiency. Through a potent combination of syrup, pills, weed, coke, and sometimes heroin—I found out soon enough that heroin and syrup in combination made me throw up *violently*—I navigated my days and nights on autopilot. Hell, with all the experimentation I did, I should have qualified for a PhD in chemistry.

My mood swings were extreme. *Getting high* meant exactly that: a heightened state of sensory perception and leeriness. Coke did that for me. In contrast, the effects of syrup or downers were soporific. A couple of slugs of Robitussin, Benalyn, Tussionex, or any of the other brands found at syrup houses all over the 'hood, combined with a handful of pills, usually 500 mg downers, turned me into a virtual zombie—unconscious but still moving. We called this *sleep-walking*, and I sleep-walked my way through large tracts of my youth.

Emerging from a nod one day, I discovered all the jewelry I'd been wearing was missing. Yup, Wenny had struck again. For all of the conflict Wiz and I went through, one of the reasons I loved him then, and remember him with gratitude right up to today, is that by teaching me all the dirty tricks in the book—and using them on me every chance he got—he helped shape me into one of the *sharpest* guys in Chicago!

True to form, he denied any responsibility for slipping the rings right off my fingers. But this time, a neighborhood girl had been sitting on the porch when it went down and had seen it all. Wiz's cover was *blown*. I confronted him again, and he looked me in the eye without flinching, feigning outraged innocence. I threatened to call in Tanzie, and seeing the game was up, Wiz flipped the script:

"*Nigga,* you ain't got to call her! Here's yo' shit! *Man,* I told you to stop noddin'. You gotta *stop* drinking that syrup for your own damn good, nigga!"

His motives may have been suspect, but Wiz wasn't wrong. My entire system had become the front line in a war between armies of uppers and downers. That's how my coke habit started—as a counterbalance to the dulling down effects of all the other stuff I swallowed. *Go figure.* The senselessness of the situation didn't pass me by either, and the internal chorus got louder:

What the fuck! You're doing this just to stay awake?

Hello, Burrel! Hello!

Just leave it be, man, just leave it alone...

The final straw came during a night out with my cousin Willy Brown. He'd been hanging around the store with me that evening, and after shutting shop, we went over to his apartment to chill out in front of the TV and to get high.

Willy was *hardcore.* He liked to shoot heroin rather than snort it, a far more potent and addictive method of absorbing the drug. While he took his half-gram, I nodded off, still working the syrup. I sensed rather than felt him fumbling with my arm, and somewhere deep in the fog of my rosy, syrup-stupor, alarm bells jangled.

I roused myself enough to register that Willy, in a bid to *share the joy,* was about to inject me with a hit of heroin. A full set of paraphernalia lay out in front of him, the needle loaded and poised. I'd come within a hair's breadth of the most deadly fix of my young life. Shocked to the core, my reaction was almost visceral. This wake-up call proved to be pivotal on my path to rehabilitation.

I never told my father what Willy had nearly done. Burrel Senior may well have killed him, a righteous fury that was pretty hard to justify considering my dad's own steady progression into serious addiction. As I clawed my way out of the abyss, my old man was free-falling into its yawning, cold, black maw.

CHAPTER NINE

A Hell Of A Year

1983 (Age 16 Years)

A Tough Separation

I WAS SIXTEEN YEARS OLD GOING ON FORTY. I'd accumulated millions of dollars and finally reached the point where it was time to turn my life all the way around, time to leave this destructive lifestyle behind. My mind, body, and heart were finally ready.

After my close encounter with the sharp point of Willy's needle, I resolved to give up all drugs except for weed. It was a tough transition, though not as brutal as I'd expected, nor as harsh as I deserved. I locked my brain onto the target, and using every ounce of will and strength I could muster, I *snapped* the chains.

When I broke free of the habit of drinking syrup and snorting coke, I finally understood that, for me, that's exactly what it had been: a *habit*, not an *addiction*. I was one of the lucky ones. I understand today how blessed I am. There are multitudes of people the world over who, with far less provocation, are destined to fight inner demons for the rest of their natural life spans. A battle the majority will lose.

It was challenging to move away from products I'd been consuming for years; to ignore their easy availability, resist *intense* peer pressure, and break free of the whole "narcotic culture," but it was a challenge I was capable of winning. My thick head, even thicker hide, and bullish stubbornness now served me well.

I conducted endless internal debates: counseling, questioning, and preparing myself mentally for the final break. I'd get frustrated and angry and was the only guy I knew who physically kicked his *own ass*! Determined to get clean of the hard stuff, I still smoked a joint or two for relaxation. Soon weed, along with a glass or two of champagne, were my only vices. In the great scheme of things, these were vices I felt I could live with.

I'd moved away from *using* hard drugs; now I needed to break away from *selling* them. To do this, all ties with the Vice Lords had to be severed. This was *not* going to be easy. When you rise to the position I held—the chief of a crew of thousands—you don't just march into someone's office one morning and hand in a letter of resignation.

Each day, thousands of guys looked to me for their livelihood. I was the one who made it possible for *them* to make the *twos and fews* they *needed* every day, to get by. By pulling the plug on Buddy Burrel, I would be pulling the plug on them, too. Violent backlash was a real possibility. I knew I had to find a way to *finesse* my departure from this gang that had been my family for nearly eight years.

My plan was simple but *cunning*! By appearing to become increasingly unpredictable, unreliable, and eccentric, I would gradually disconnect myself from day-to-day operations, and slowly *slide* out of the overall picture. In the end, everyone would breathe a sigh of relief.

South Side Socialites

A new dimension to my social life was to prove a useful tool in my plan: I was dating *South Side* women. In my neighborhood, South Side women were considered sophisticated and classy. Usually, they wouldn't be seen dead with a *nigga* from our side of the fence. West Side guys were viewed as hardcore and uncouth, too rough around the edges for more refined tastes.

Smart and self-assured, I had the confidence and maturity of a man *many* years older, and I had *style*, qualities that played well, South, East, West, *or* North. To me, it was natural to hang with *chicks*, who may be older in calendar years, but were intellectually and emotionally in tune with me. Soon I was experiencing the heady delights of being taken in hand by some very elegant, classy, and *worldly* women.

My personal education in this unorthodox "finishing school" continued in the company, and arms, of some of the South Side's finest grand dames, and I was having the *time of my life*. Attending all kinds of topflight functions, frequenting the finest Rush Street restaurants, and even going to the theater, I felt my sophistication barometer rising each day. Back in the 'hood, in the meantime, I was noticeably MIA.

To add to the perception that I was heading off the rails, I changed my entire look, *radically*. I started wearing fatigues all day, every day, until they became my trademark. I had a hell of a look going, and even in a neighborhood where the eccentricities and extremes of *pimp fashion* were commonplace, folks thought I'd gone crazy!

Striding around, camouflaged from head to toe, heavy-soled combat boots drumming the pavement and layers of gold and diamond chains around my neck, clanking like cow-bells, you'd *hear* me coming long before you'd *see* me. A hunting knife strapped to my arm and another to my ankle, I had all kinds of jungle-survival paraphernalia hanging from my belt—pretty rich considering the only greenery I *ever* got close to was in my dad's garden, the grocery store, or a spliff!

Handing Down My Rank

Reaction to my *unpredictability* was, of course, *predictable*. Initially, people were happy enough to screw me out of my share of the takings—if I wasn't there to pull my weight, I sure as hell wasn't getting any of the rewards. But soon there were too many unresolved problems sitting on the back burner and open decisions cluttering up the in-tray. Resentment simmered then bubbled. A snide remark here and there, unofficial meetings, and huddled, hushed conversations in corners, it was clear frustration was turning into antipathy. If the situation weren't soon resolved, events would probably turn ugly, fast.

The command structure in any "political" organization, no matter how apparently stable, is usually dynamic. Even the most confident and established leader can spot any number of *pretenders to the throne*, just by looking over his shoulder. They may nod, smile, and swear they've got his back, but the hunger in their eyes tells a different story. Take me to meet any crew, and in a second, I'll point out which young bucks are quietly preparing their bid for the crown.

Sooner rather than later, my authority as chief would be openly challenged. There was no avoiding it. The problem had to be confronted head-on, and in order to extract myself with my status—and health—intact, it was essential I keep the upper hand.

Convening a powwow with senior crew members, I told them straight, that changes had to be made. Torn between the demands of my father—who had reeled me back into his business and reinstated me as his right-hand man—and my mistresses, I said, I felt I had no choice but to take a break from the CIVLs.

My story was credible. I'd paved the way well, and as with all the best alibis, mine contained more than a few grains of truth. Burrel Senior was recognized far and wide as a serious *playa* with a *fearsome* temper. It was also common knowledge that I was messing with sophisticated South Side women, my moves up the social ladder watched with more than a little envy.

At the end of the day, it was evident that the CIVL leadership clique *needed* to buy my story in order to provide us all with a way out of this impasse. Tired of my inconsistency, eccentricity, and unreliability, they just wanted *shot* of me. I'd driven the wedge in between us too deeply for it to be removed. But could they afford to let me go?

Well, the timing was good. There were few practical advantages to keeping me on as "Board Chairman." In the early days of operations, my involvement had been critical for sourcing merchandise, a key link in the chain between my father's supplies and us. But Burrel Senior's connections were no longer useful. Rich new channels had been opened, and I'd distanced myself from it all.

The ghetto is fuelled, greased, and ignited by greed. It wasn't difficult then, to manipulate these dynamics to serve my own interests. In short order, I passed my Vice Lord rank down to some of my thirstier lieutenants, and like an empty bottle under a running tap, the leadership vacuum was quickly filled to overflowing.

It wasn't quite over though. Tensions still sputtered and occasionally flared. I continued to hang around with some of the older guys I'd come to know well during my street career, guys who for the most part were affiliated with different crews. For a while, I was suspected by some of my old Vice Lord buddies of shifting allegiance and turning my back on my brothers: a potentially incendiary situation that could become conflagration in a second, if ignited by a stray spark of rumor.

The streets are ruthless and uncompromising. A guy will be shut down, assassinated, simply because that's easier than trying to figure him out. Why take the risk of leaving a flank open when you can protect it with a well-placed bullet?

Mistrust, suspicion, and jealousy are all but tangible in the ghetto, and sensitive to the time bomb on which we were all sitting, I had to negotiate my way out with care. I spent countless hours explaining to these guys that I really *was* getting out of this game, and they should be pleased for me. After all, I was only doing what *everyone* dreamed about.

Trust me when I tell you, there's not a guy on the streets, or in the penitentiary, who hasn't promised himself at some point that one fine day, he'll move on from this life. He'll make a fresh start, he swears, for his family and himself, in business, or in another 'hood, or in a different state. It's what we *all* talked about *all the time.* Buried deep in the psyche of every guy I ever knew—even the most hardened of criminals—was the dream of one day leaving *all this behind.*

But few succeed. A deadly soup of power, status, money, drugs, and sex, each as addictive as the next, the streets are multi-tentacled. You wriggle out from under one and find yourself tangled up in another. It's a hard place, and mind-set, to escape. Peer pressure firmly anchors you down but should you succeed in breaking away, it's likely that the weight of "sins-already-committed" will suck you right back in. Just like the Al Pacino movie *Carlito's Way,* the road *out* is littered with *one-last-favors* and *one-last-times.*

But I was getting out. Now was the right time, I knew, to re-brand myself. With little ado, *Buddy Burrel*, gang chief, dealer, user, and street hustler was laid to rest—and *The King* was born.

" Burrel is a player, and a player runs rings around a gang-banger. The gang-banger is about brute force, but the player knows chess; he's a strategist. This is Burrel's great skill, which enabled him to survive so long in this environment, to move out of it, and to get where he is today. He's a heck of a chess player... "

—Big C

Coming of Age

My sixteenth birthday was a *hell* of a day. It was the day I officially left the streets *and* left home, moving out of my parent's house after a stand-off with Dad.

It was May 6, 1983, and I should have been mowing the lawn. Chores were chores, no exceptions made for birthdays. But I couldn't face it. Instead, I spent the day with a chick I knew, chilling and counting my cash reserves. Even as I pushed the inevitability of Dad's retribution firmly to the back of my mind, I think I knew we were heading for our final showdown.

I was sixteen years old, a battle-hardened adult, a father, and, by anyone's standards, a wealthy man. With multimillions of dollars stashed away, I had the means to do anything I wanted. But all the money in the world didn't change the fact that I'd be in *deep shit* when I got home.

There were good and bad aspects to living under my father's wing. I had a great pad, was surrounded by a family I loved, and blended in well with my father's business dealings. But I wasn't a free agent, and my dad made sure I didn't forget it for a second.

His mental games and physical punishments had worn me down to the nub. His compulsive need for total control was exhausting. Whether facing endless lists of demeaning chores, listening to him constantly throwing Wenny in my face, or harping on about how much I owed him, the whole routine had become a tired old record. I was at the end of my rope.

Over and over the same angry rehearsal ran through my head: "*You wanna play like that, Dad? Well, I'll show you! I don' have to fuck with you no more! I'm gonna to do my own thing. Yeah, gonna do my own fuckin' thing.*"

By the time I headed for home, I'd psyched myself up into a lather of outrage and defiance. Dad was in the front-yard, slowly and deliberately raking up the last remains of winter debris.

He looked the same to me as he had when I was six years old; stern, strong, and capable of snapping my arm in two should he choose to. But I wasn't six any longer, and I know the young man, striding down the street toward him, must have given him pause. I was, after all, a reflection of him. To my ears, the pounding of my heart sounded louder than the tattoo of my heavy boots on the pavement. Sweat tricked down my back; beads of perspiration dotted my forehead. But I didn't, for a second, take my eyes from his face.

He stopped moving, leaned on the wooden handle of his rake, and watched me walk toward him.

Even in that moment, I believe we both knew it was over. But old habits die hard, and as soon as I was in hearing distance, he started in on me: "If you gonna live in my *fuckin'* house, you live by *my fuckin' rules*, junior." His face was pinched with fury.

"I know Dad . . ."

"I don' care how much man you think you is *boy*," he spat on the grass in contempt, "you ain't no *fuckin' man* until you got your own fuckin' place."

I took a deep breath: "I got my own place."

He didn't answer.

"Gonna be the man you taught me to be, Dad."

"When you leavin'?"

"Today."

"A 'right."

He looked sideways at me then. "You still gotta place here."

"Yeah. But I got no plans on comin' back."

"I know it, Junior."

With that, Dad went back to raking the garden.

And that was that. With a mixture of trepidation, regret, and exhilaration, I went inside, packed my clothes and some cash I'd been storing, and left Cortez Street. The future promised a combination of *liberation* and *liability*. Whatever fuck-ups I made from hereon would be mine, and mine alone.

As it transpired, my leaving home was a seminal event for both my father and me. From that day on, our paths diverged sharply. For me, it marked the start of an extraordinary chapter of personal growth, while for Burrel Senior it proved to be a watershed moment in what would be a decade-long story of declining fortunes.

BL's Fall from Grace

Now well into his forties, my father had been using narcotics heavily since his early twenties. With the constitution of an ox and extraordinarily high tolerance thresholds, he sometimes consumed drugs, nonstop, for up to three or four days at a time. I'll never understand how his body coped with the huge infusions of chemicals and herbs it was subjected to, each day.

Dad had given up his "respectable job" as a sanitation worker a few years earlier, and now his days were spent either dealing, using, or engaged in some small-scale pimping. Dad's idea of pimping was to muscle in on some working girls' corners, and take a share of the action. Even though he socialized with some of Chicago's most powerful and infamous pimps—characters like Bishop Don Juan and Godfather—he never developed a taste for the business, nor the patience required to run it.

These days Burrel Senior was doing a lot less dealing and a lot more consuming. It used to be that marijuana was enough to keep him mellow, then came cocaine and the deadly addictiveness of heroin. Over the next few years, Dad went from being a straight, hardcore businessman, to hanging out with the wilder elements of the West Side. He appeared to have hit a classic male mid-life crisis, although his played out a little differently from those of the average suburban, middle-aged male.

Burrel Senior enjoyed spending time with the brash, young Puerto Rican kids who ran a number of flourishing operations around the Humboldt Park area. Cash-rich, they were happy to spend it and sure knew how to have a good time. My old man developed a taste for Puerto Rican chicks. The heady mix of business, recreation, salsa, and sex readily available around these young Latinos proved irresistible—and every bit as addictive as narcotics. These kids gave him respect, too, so he got to make money, get laid, party, and play God all at the same time.

When his long, downhill odyssey started, Dad had been sitting on millions of dollars in cash. Even with business declining, he lived comfortably off this stockpiled fortune for another eight or nine years. But his cash wasn't being recycled. These days it was all heading one way, out of *his* pocket and into someone *else's*.

One by one, assets were liquidated to pay for his habits. When I was about nineteen, my father decided he was fed up with putting money and effort into the upkeep of the B&C Grocery and sold the store. The business empire Burrel Senior had planned, worked for, and built from the back of a garbage truck was fast turning to dust.

It was as though my dad and I had swapped roles. He was living out his forties the way I'd lived out my early teens: on the streets dealing with *punks*. As I moved away from drug addiction and street life, my dad was succumbing to it. In the end, he voluntarily lowered himself into the quicksand from which I'd fought so hard to extricate myself.

We passed each other on the way.

Together Alone

My old man continued to lose stature and dignity. Mixing with small fry, he fed his addictions until he was just another junkie. Instead of growing, he diminished a little more each day. Now and again, he'd sell a little product, but would try to stretch it out by cutting it with low-quality crap. His reputation was dismantled far faster than it was built. Soon he was his own best, and only, customer.

My mom finally found the courage to leave my father when I was nineteen. With Marcel and Tweety in tow, she moved in with her brother Larry. My dad's temper tantrums and his mental and physical abusiveness gave her the reason; his persistent self-destructiveness the opportunity.

Still, it took *enormous* courage for Gloria to cut ties and move out. I'd always said I would stand by my mom when she decided to leave my father, and I was as good as my word.

My father, furious and bitter, gave her *nothing* to live on. As far as he was concerned, Gloria was on her own financially, yet she still *belonged* to him in some sense. He started harassing, phoning, threatening, begging, and demeaning her. He was playing the same cruel mind games that, in fact, had driven her out of the relationship. It came to a head when he told her that if he wasn't to have her, no one would. He told her that he had put a *hit* out on her. She wouldn't even see it coming, he said.

It was time to intervene. I went to visit Dad, looked him straight in the eye and told him: if he ever, *ever* came near or hassled Mom again, I would take his legs off at the knees, followed by his head, and *then* I'd kick his ass. He looked back at me, saw the truth in my eyes, and *never* bothered her again. It was the final transfer of power.

Cortez Street became a bachelor pad, a boys' club. I was sharing an apartment in Oak Park with Wenny at this time—continuing our love-hate relationship—but I'd go visit Dad whenever I was conducting business in his neighborhood. We'd sit in the garden, smoke, speculate, and share homespun philosophy and conspiracy theories, and over time, we found a level of companionship we'd failed to achieve while living under the same roof.

Still, as time went on and Burrel Senior's fortunes and self-respect continued their downward spiral, I found the situation tougher to cope with. Angry and frustrated, I just didn't understand why one of the smoothest, coolest, most respected operators in Chicago was letting his life trickle through his fingers, like sand.

This wasn't the same man I'd idolized, loved, and feared for so many years. Where was the fight? I tried to shock him into taking action and stop the rot, but nothing I did had much impact. My dad had always been his own man, and there was to be no sudden *moment of clarity* to propel him back on track.

He might have continued to get by, treading water—and keeping his nose just above it—but for a dreadful day in 1991 when he heard that Charles Selvey, his brother and lifelong buddy, had overdosed.

Uncle Charles

Uncle Charles was part of the family though he wasn't really my dad's brother, nor by extension my uncle. Charles was actually BL's first cousin, but they were as close as brothers could be. They'd grown up in the same house in Mississippi and had as complex a relationship as any two brothers.

My dad was the oldest and a lot tougher than Charles. To prove it, he'd regularly kick Charles's ass, and as kids, they were always scrapping. The hierarchy, established way back then, stood the test of time, and although they fought like cat and dog for the next three decades, they were as close as two pages in a book.

Moving to Chicago around the same time, they gravitated toward different neighborhoods but still saw each other often. Uncle Charles invariably infuriated my father. Fair-skinned and even-featured, he was considered to be a good-looking guy. Cool, even arrogant, on the outside, his confident demeanor hid the soft underbelly of a *ladies man*. Charles's nose was *always* open for the fairer sex. He loved women with a passion and charmed his way into the heads, hearts, and underwear of more than a few. It seemed to us kids that he was perpetually entangled in one situation or another, involving an angry woman; her husband, boyfriend, father; or, of course, his own wife.

Road Trip Heaven

When I think of Charles, I mostly remember the road trips. Our extended family straddled the country from Mississippi to Chicago. Some soul or another was usually in transit from this world to the next, and respects needed to be paid. Though it was mostly funerals rather than family reunions that took us back down South, as often as not they turned into one and the same.

I just loved those trips!

Puffed up with excitement, I'd bustle around importantly, as our prodigal family loaded up their Cadillacs with food, drink, wives, kids, and old battered suitcases, and readied to head for home. We never departed during daylight. By leaving at eleven or twelve at night, we'd miss the worst of the traffic and keep a low profile—well, as low a profile as a gaudy convoy of Cadillacs *brimful* with Chicago gangsters could ever hope to keep. Night driving reduced the risk, too, of being caught smoking the spliffs which burned incessantly en route, filling the cars with sweet, green fug.

For us youngsters, it was the *best* treat you could imagine. Invariably chaotic and disorganized, we'd somehow get ourselves on the road after what seemed like hours of noisy preparation. You could bet your fortune that only a few minutes later, we'd be stopping at a gas station for fuel, to use the lavatories, or to buy some soda. The Cadis were gas-guzzlers, and we'd have to stop often on the 850-mile journey to refuel. The smaller the town, the greater our *shock value!* Locals would scatter in front of us, or stop dead in their tracks glued to the spot, jaws dropping in horror. They'd gawk at this bunch of flashy, loud Chi-town gangsters in their tailor-mades and jangling chains as though we were some kind of exotic, but dangerous, species of wildlife, which I suppose, in some respects, we were.

There'd be any number of fights, squabbles, punctures, and accidents along the way, but no matter how protracted the journey, as soon as we got there, most of us kids wanted to turn *right around* and head straight back home. All that greenery, cow shit, and mud, not to mention the damn *mosquitoes!* For urban rats like us, the *journey* was always way better than the destination.

Lives Unravel

On the surface, Uncle Charles was pretty square. He'd never lived on the West Side but had migrated south. That already set him apart from us. South Side neighborhoods were considered very *bugie,* or upscale, compared to the West, one of the very reasons I regularly headed that way to hook up with desirable women. With his good job, his large suburban house, and smart wife, Charles was living the dream. True to ghetto-form, rather than *celebrate* his success, we preferred to *dissect* it. To us, it seemed as though Charles thought he was better than everyone else, and that *wasn't* cool.

He was certainly a hypocrite. While he berated my father for the way he was raising me, holding up his own children as role models, Charles's own narcotics use and profligate womanizing were conveniently swept under the rug. And even as he forged his way through the shop floor at the Ford plant to the position of senior supervisor, he used his unique access and connections to distribute drugs to the two thousand-strong factory workforce.

But at the end of the day, most of our resentment was fuelled by what we saw as the disparagement of *our* way of life, implied by the way he chose to live *his.*

Charles's fortunes plummeted, in the mid-eighties, when his wife finally left him, taking with her the children and just about everything else that wasn't nailed down. She eventually agreed to move back in, as long as Charles moved *out*. He agreed and moved from the suburban dream into a first floor West Side apartment owned by my dad.

He and Burrel Senior began hanging out again, just like the old days. This, as it transpired, wasn't healthy for either of them: each was a bad influence on the other. Burrel Senior led Charles, already on a steep downhill incline, even further astray, and Charles, in turn, became BL's reliable "get high" buddy. They went to bed with getting high on their minds and woke up just to make it happen.

Charles was so spaced out these days it was a wonder he could hold down his job, although the discipline of working in a highly regulated corporate environment forced him to keep his wits about him to a degree and probably slowed his decline. When the closure of the Ford plant was announced, it was catastrophic for him, professionally and personally.

I've seen it happen a thousand times, but am still staggered at just how rapidly lives can disintegrate. For Charles, the lifestyle he'd been so proud of simply *combusted*. In less than twelve months, he went from respectable, suburban, middle-class family man to drug-dependent, broke, unemployed lodger. He'd never find his way back.

Dad continued to mess with the streets, swallow or snort anything he could lay his hands on, and fight with Charles. Their relationship was turbulent. Charles was always doing something to upset Burrel Senior, cutting some side-deal or shooting his mouth off, but it was still probably the worst day of Dad's life when his friend died.

There was always speculation about how and why it happened. The rumor mill was in full swing, and the air thick with stories of suicide, manslaughter, and conspiracy. It doesn't matter if the location is suburbia, the corridors of a large corporation, or the ghetto, gossip greases the wheels. Fingers were pointed mostly at Camala—Charles's unfortunate girlfriend—and for weeks following his death, tongues wagged incessantly.

I've always believed it was exactly what it appeared to be: a tragic mistake. There was no conspiracy. Charles accidentally self-administered a last, lethal fix and died an ignominious and premature death. But I believe, too, that he'd lost all hope. He'd been suffering from depression for some time, and though I've no way of knowing, I can't help but speculate that he may have welcomed the chance to lay down his load. Who knows? Maybe at the end Charles knew exactly what he was doing.

My dad took it hard, though, hard as *hell*. It all but killed him on the inside. Charles and he had been running and sparring partners their entire lives, and Charles's terrible death carved a slice out of Dad's soul. He seemed to stop caring that day; it was as though he suddenly burnt out. His decline accelerated, and when he was arrested in a drug house a few years later, I didn't bail him out for over two months. If he was forced to sober up, I rationalized, then maybe he'd *wake up* and *wise up*.

Eventually he did, but it took many more years before he hit rock bottom, and it would take his mother to give him a reason to haul himself up by the scruff of his neck. Back in Mississippi, she owned the family small holding. She told her son, in no uncertain terms, that he wouldn't get a *sniff* of it, as long as he continued to get high.

Seeing no other path ahead except a steep one down to his grave, Burrel Senior played his last ticket. Going cold turkey, he packed his bags and headed home.

CHAPTER TEN

The Night Shift

1984–1985 (Age 17–18 Years)

24/7

SIXTEEN FLOWED INTO SEVENTEEN, and 1984 continued to be my busiest year so far. It might also have been classified as my most *absurd*.

I'd successfully broken away from a destructive, hard-drug habit; had separated myself physically and emotionally from the streets; and perhaps most importantly of all, had put distance between my old man and me. I was sitting on great deal of cash and, though undecided as to what I would do with it, was enjoying weighing my options. Life was looking good.

Then like a thunderbolt out of the blue I was forced to get a job! Yup, a time card-punching, uniform-wearing, seven-bucks-an-hour kind of job. This had *not* been factored into my master plan.

Here's how it came about: It was the Thanksgiving holiday, and I was out and about with my baby's mom, Pam, and her brother Tony. Completely out of the game by now, I was relaxed and feeling good. We took a drive—a spin along the lakeshore—in Tony's new Seville, for no reason other than the pleasure of the ride. Though it was late autumn, it was a glorious day. The sky was blue, the air was crisp and fresh, and sunshine glittered on water like finely cut white diamonds. The whole picture had the feel of an old Technicolor movie, just a little *too* bright, but lavishly beautiful. We hit one of those odd lulls that sometimes occur on highways in the midst of holiday mayhem, and the road stretched ahead of us, mouthwateringly clear.

Tony floored the pedal, and we let *rip*. That's when the cop car slotted in behind us, lights flashing and sirens squealing like a stuck pig. Tony freaked out. He'd been stopped for speeding a few weeks earlier, he said, and had his license suspended. He faced the prospect of losing it permanently should he be caught driving. I had a couple of joints in a bag on the backseat, but in all honesty, didn't expect any *twisters* to go to the trouble of searching us on such an innocuous, sunny holiday afternoon— not with all the paperwork *that* would probably entail.

I made a split-second decision and, as we pulled ahead of the police car, rashly offered to exchange places with Tony and take the wheel. Without word or hesitation, he pulled over. We switched seats in a blink and waited by the side of the road.

Close enough on our tails to have seen the seat-exchange, the cop came to the window, asked for my license, and demanded to know why we'd swapped places. I usually brazened my way through situations like these, and passionately denied we'd done any such thing. The officer shrugged, looked at me with evident exasperation, and moved on to the usual formalities. Imagine my surprise when the first unit called for backup; the car was searched from roof to chassis, and a kilo of cocaine was uncovered in the cavity under the spare wheel!

I emerged from a lengthy court process with eighteen-months probation stretching ahead of me like a dreary, waterless desert.

One of my great strengths is my adaptability, however, and I quickly, though begrudgingly, adjusted to this new reality. It wasn't the end of the world after all. As long as I made it to the weekly meetings scheduled at the probation office in Markham, I rationalized, it needn't cramp my style at all. Wrong.

Debbie, my probation officer, was a piece of work: humorless; frustrated by a low-paying, thankless job; and *real cranky!* At the time, I thought she was vindictive, but in hindsight, I have to admit that she was just one *shrewd* lady. She had my measure right off. But then again, I wasn't particularly subtle. After a few weeks of watching me sashay into her office—dripping with diamonds—and then sashay out again to jump into one waiting luxury car or another, she called a halt.

"*Get a job,*" she ordered.

I sniggered.

She looked at me combatively. "If I don't see a pay-stub from you in the next two weeks, add another eighteen months to your probation."

I glared.

She glared back.

"You think I'm joking, Burrel? *Just try me out!*"

Reilly, my friend and lawyer, confirmed the next day that she had all the power she needed to follow through on her threat. I was left facing, what to me, was a *horrifying* prospect. I had to find a job, and frankly, I didn't know where to start!

As usual, it was Mom who came through.

Arriving home from work a few days after my conversation with Debbie, she told me she'd called in a favor from her supervisor at the hospital. I could start there the next day, as a salaried employee, working the night shift.

Now this was really *something* coming from my mom. A constant, gentle presence, she'd quietly watched me *fuck up* my whole life. She loved me unconditionally, but I knew I'd broken her heart a hundred times over. My dilemma presented her with one, too: she didn't want me on extended probation, but neither did she want me causing trouble in the workplace that represented her "alternative world," her sanctuary.

It was never really a fair fight, though, and as usual, her kind heart won out. I embarked on an unexpected new career cutting my teeth as a patient transporter at the Illinois Masonic, working the eleven p.m. to seven a.m. night shift, four times a week.

Night work didn't really bother me. There was quite a bit of physical labor involved, but it wasn't too arduous for a strong, young guy like me. My responsibilities included moving sick patients—some with advanced terminal illnesses—around the hospital, delivering night meds, and transporting dead bodies to the morgue. A lot of folks die at night, and I didn't have a problem with any one of them—it's the live ones who'd always given me grief.

I was surprisingly good at my job. I promised my mom I'd keep a low profile and wouldn't flash my status, but couldn't stop myself from buying twenty custom uniforms, tailored to fit *just so*. I was always clean, crisp, and creased. Once I'd wrapped my brain around the idea that this was the way it was going to be for awhile, I buckled down and just got on with it. I worked hard but was sometimes so exhausted from my daytime activities, that forty winks in a broom closet was required!

It's fair to say, the manner in which I spent my daylight hours *couldn't* have been further removed from these sterile nights of disinfectant, bedpans, and bodies.

Property Magnate

I'd acquired a taste for property development from my father. Buying property made sense as a means of laundering money, building equity, and securing a regular flow of income. My first purchases were a couple of apartment blocks on the West Side. I had a pretty sweet formula. Through my political connections, I'd pick up a decrepit apartment building for a song, rehab it, and before too long, have a decent rent-roll going. Soon I had a substantial stable of property.

My apartments had a distinct fingerprint and were always recognizable as "King Burrel buildings." They sported large picture-framed windows, light beige sandblasted exteriors with neat, dark pointing, and bright, well-decorated interiors. I rented mostly to professionals: teachers, government workers, and nurses. These folks would have solid credit, I rationalized, and would be good payers. Both assumptions were wrong. Many of these hard-working, square-job folks were struggling to keep their heads above water. Before long, I had more arrears than rent-roll.

I soon got weary of the whole rigmarole. Folks didn't pay their rent; I'd try and evict them, and, before I knew it, I'd be hauled up in court to defend myself. I decided it was time to clear the decks and focus only on new construction. From now on, it was strictly buying and selling for me. So when another speculator, a guy called Brian, offered to buy all eighteen buildings from me as a block, I agreed without hesitation, selling the lot for somewhere between $7 million and $8 million.

Welcome to the Burbs

Old Oak Brook is a jewel in the crown of Chicago suburbia. This quiet, wooded backwater, west of Chicago, looks like a natural but well-tended garden. Manicured, lush, and reeking of wealth, Old Oak Brook has a classier character than some more established, densely populated suburbs. It's a place that appeals to the kind of man who doesn't want to follow the crowd; a man seeking a low profile; a man, in fact, like me, a refugee from the ghetto. Old Oak Brook, nestled deep in the heart of respectability, seemed like a perfect hideaway to me.

If you turn off Ogden and drive along the winding, leafy tunnel of Spring Road, you'll arrive at Natoma Drive. This exclusive little enclave was my new 'hood, but, unfortunately, as it transpired, my ability to lay low was *zero*.

I can only imagine what the neighbors thought as I arrived and they watched the foundations of my new home begin to take shape. I was a constant and colorful presence: driving back and forth in various vehicles, supervising the work, dressed in full combat gear (my fatigues blended nicely with the foliage fringing our elegant cul-de-sac), and sporting enough gold around my neck to keep Tutenkamen happy.

The house was a beauty. The architectural plans were based on a limited edition Ralph Lauren Polo design. It was to be 15,000 square feet of spectacularly designed, pure self-indulgence. It was the home I'd always dreamed of. Money was no object, although I had to find creative ways to freshen my funds. There would be no skimping on this baby!

Four floors in all—three on top and one below—the structure sat deceptively low on the ground. As you walked up the path, you passed between twin stone lions. Poised and proud, they guarded an enormous entrance. You entered the marble-clad foyer set, like a deep blue lagoon in the embrace of twin spiral staircases, that spilled out in front of you. If you followed this marble river through to the back of the house, you'd enter the pool area.

The full-size pool was my pride and joy, even though I could only swim vertically! One half of this little slice of the Caribbean was constructed outside the main building; the other half was fully covered and inside. That made it ideal for all-weather pool parties and a tropical oasis, during those *long, freezing* Chicago winters. The indoor section was separated from its outer half by an underwater grid, which, when opened, allowed you to swim into the glittering, open-air pool and patio area. The circular bar and attendant stools in the center of the pool became the focal point for more than one wild party. The gazebo with hot tub, sitting at the rear of the patio area, like a sentinel, was a great perch from which to watch the action, and I spent many happy hours immersed in its bubbles and steam, glass of champagne in hand.

Back inside the house was much more to explore. Six master suites, two kitchens, eight bathrooms, and hot tubs galore. Everywhere you turned, steel, marble, glass, and spotlights glittered brightly. The air was infused with the perfume of fresh-cut flowers. My weekly standing order for elaborate, seasonal flower arrangements ratcheted up bills that ran to thousands of dollars each month.

The soft furnishings were no less lavish. I purchased fine European furniture, by the truckload, from the famous Rossi Brothers Store in Chicago. Specializing in high-end furniture, it was a classy and expensive joint. Most of the bigwigs I knew went there, and what was good for *them* was certainly good for me. By the time the Old Oak Brook house was fully furnished and fitted, I'd spent the best part of $700,000 with the brothers Rossi, creating an ultramodern showcase of a home. The experience indirectly led me, many years later, to open up my own fine furnishings store.

When all was said and done, though, the finest feature of the house was one that few people would ever see. Beneath the kitchen floor, deep in a cavity below the ceramic tiles, several custom-built steel cases were buried. Each held millions of dollars of *going nowhere* money, entombed during the construction process. There was no easy access to these funds. To reach them, I'd have to smash the tiles and dig up the floor. No, this money represented long-term security, and I had no intention of unearthing a *single dollar* unless *forced* to do so. And I couldn't see why that should ever happen.

During the construction process, eyeballs popped and tongues wagged throughout the neighborhood. In the days following my move into my magnificent new home, you could almost hear a collective "*hisssssss*" of dismay rippling through the trees of the local Fullenburg Woods.

Apart from the waves of visitors making their way up my drive—

predominantly large black guys with loud clothes and even louder jewelry—it was the cars that turned heads. Within a few months of arriving in Old Oak Brook, I owned seventeen vehicles; Rolls Royces, Mercedes, Corvettes, and Mustangs rotated through the five-car garage or were parked along the snaking driveway.

I was living the dream.

If You Can Dream It . . .

Like so many other black kids, I frequently daydreamed my way down the section of Lake Shore Drive that converges so sweetly with downtown Chicago. For many years, this was a favorite pastime. Cruising along with the top and windows down and a couple of buddies at my side, we enjoyed the warm summer nights best of all, made all the more precious because there were so few. We'd crank up the music until Frank Sinatra or Michael Franks was blasting from the speakers with enough force to lift us off the road. Puffing on a joint or three, we'd meander up and down that beautiful stretch of highway, admiring the city's dramatic profile.

I loved the brick and stucco *white-glove* buildings that formed one boundary of the S-Curve, a sweeping arc of road stretching from North Lake Shore to East, hugging water, beaches, and city. These dignified and stately apartments dominated the skyline, standing shoulder to shoulder, their banks of bright, unblinking eyes reflected on a black patent leather lake. This neighborhood was home to some *serious* old money.

We'd stop, get out, and sit down with our backs to the water, leaning back far enough, to be able to gaze upwards without cricking our necks. Picking out the penthouses, we'd imagine what it would be like to live in one of those *palaces in the sky.*

When those big, high-ceiling apartments were lit up from the inside, you might catch a glimpse of a flickering TV screen, the movement of people, or the glitter of a majestic glass chandelier. We wove stories by the dozen and dreamed out loud. What great parties we'd throw and what fine hosts we'd be! What beautiful women we'd have on our arms, how much Cristal champagne we'd drink, and how *everyone* would look at us with envy.

It took me years to understand that those mind-pictures I painted hadn't really been about *owning* an apartment on Lake Shore Drive at all. Rather those balmy storytelling evenings had reflected a deep hankering to be the *kind of man* who inhabited one of those elegant, status-conscious buildings. I yearned to be a man of stature and substance, respected and accepted by other powerful people.

Even as a young gang chief, I aspired to be more than Buddy Burrel, leader on my block. I wanted to be a *leader of men*. Unable to articulate it in words, I *dreamed* it instead.

> *You know, anything I ever heard Burrel talk about, I saw materialize. I watched it all unfold just the way he said it would. Even the things I thought impossible.*
> —Messiah

Party Central

On the surface, it would appear as though I operated in two irreconcilable worlds. On the one hand, I was a respectable and respected property developer and, on the other, a hospital porter wheeling dead bodies around the Illinois Masonic several nights a week.

I was determined that my night-shift curfew wasn't going to cramp my networking though, and I stepped up my socializing activities to compensate for those *nonproductive* nights. I moved in different circles these days, mingling with the development community and with a number of high-powered property kings and their financial backers.

We partied hard. Dining at swanky Rush Street restaurants, later hitting a nightclub or a late night bar, for a nightcap or two. But in all honesty, there was little in the way of entertainment that really got these guys *excited*. Established Chicago nightspots were pretty conservative, and I realized that these bored wealthy men represented an underserved market. They had money to burn and couldn't find enough ways to burn it.

This was a market gap I could fill. I had the sophistication, the connections, and the facilities. I did some planning, made some calls, and, by the summer of '85, was ready to roll with the mother of all parties. It was an astounding success, and soon such boisterous bashes were regular events, twice a month, minimum, at the Old Oak Brook house.

Dozens of business associates turned up at these functions, many bringing along a friend or two. These were high-ticket, private affairs; the door fee of a hundred bucks simply got you across the threshold. Everyone entering was carefully vetted; you only got in based on personal recommendation. In this manner, we were able to keep our parties exclusive and discrete.

Inside the house, it was *wild*. Everywhere you looked beautiful women were reclining, chatting, laughing, dancing, and flirting. I invited women I'd met across the years, and they brought friends. Soon word spread to relatives and friends of friends. Over time some of the loveliest ladies in Chicago walked up that lion-flanked path to my home.

The guys who attended these parties had never experienced anything like them: the glamorous environment, the high-caliber company, the beauty and exoticness of the women, and the lavishness of the hospitality. There was nowhere else they could go, that could guarantee the same levels of security, privacy, discretion, and *fun*. Our parties may even have been raunchier than the infamous bacchanals that took place at the original Playboy mansion, located a few miles away in downtown Chicago. Hard drugs weren't allowed, but champagne flowed, joints were smoked, and music throbbed—you could all but *taste* the *frisson*.

I didn't relax for a second. Functioning as host, security, mediator, and traffic cop, I was everywhere, ensuring everyone had a good time. I didn't drink or smoke and was constantly moving among the crowd, meeting, greeting, shaking hands, and slapping backs. This was *turbonetworking*!

It was also profitable. We'd agreed that the girls would keep 50 percent of anything they made at these events. I'd take the other half, and the door fee would cover the overhead. My take from the first party, which was relatively small in comparison to the ones that followed, was more than $25,000.

The financial arrangements worked well for us all, and the future potential was clear. The girls loved it. They enjoyed the glamour and the socializing and, I suspect, got a kick out of the fact that a bunch of important, affluent men threw their dignity to the dogs and fawned over them like star-struck school kids.

Two parties a month was about our limit, as we endeavored to stay below the radar of the local neighborhood watch—and failed *spectacularly*. It was pretty hard to miss the waves of gorgeous girls, long legs, spandex, and silk as well as the suits and fine cars, moving in and out of this normally quiet little cul-de-sac. It left little room for doubt that there was some *serious* partying going down.

A stream of new faces was soon burbling its way past the lion sentinels. The local alpha-males had arrived, wishing to share some of their *concerns*. After a little probing, it was evident that the main gripe wasn't that we were throwing wild, wet, and sexy parties, but that they hadn't been *invited!* Our next few get-togethers embraced more than a smattering of local representation. The neighborhood watch had moved *poolside*.

Fallout was, of course, inevitable. There were a number of residents—notably outraged wives—who weren't about to turn a blind eye to such scandalous goings-on. Although for a while, with the complicity of more than a few suburban husbands, we were able to defuse tension. Still, local resistance ramped up and was becoming a major headache.

It was hard to imagine that angry neighbors were soon to be the *least* of my problems.

❶ Big Mike, a kingpin, and city worker. He was a man who knew how to leverage the system.

❷ Big John, my mentor and good friend. Always sharp, John talked me out of ghetto-fabulous and into Armani.

❸ Primped, proud, and ready to party. Of these guys, one is dead today, and five have done hard time.

❶ Prince Dank, Willy Lord's right-hand man; Wenny; and me.

❷ Bishop Don "Magic" Juan and General, both founding members of the Four Aces Club.

The "Four Aces" and Friends. Left to right: Cadillac, (the Club), Godfather (the Spade), Mr. T (bodyguard), Bullet (associate), Bishop Don "Magic" Juan (the Diamond), and General (the Heart).

❶ "Les girls" out in force at a party.

❷ A "Topflight" associate.

❸ Power couple, before Topflight finally disintegrated.

I was living the kind of movie star life I'd always dreamed of. Beautiful women, lots of *bling*, and endless partying at the hottest places.

❶ I was crowned King by the Four Aces who admired my coast-to-coast business expansion.

❷ Handed down through several generations, this ceremonial staff was said to have originated in Ethiopia, where it allegedly had been used to quell rebellion. Who knows? But if you look closely enough, you can see that the white chunks embedded in the sides are actual teeth!

Golfing with God. It's no
wonder—dressed like
this—we scared the heck
out of everyone when we
turned up for a round or
two!

① Red was lucky for me so I wore it often, when not wearing fatigues. Here we are at a tournament where God has just won $30,000. The expression on God's son's face says it all . . .

② We'd sometimes make as much in the car-park, with a few last minute bets, as we had all day.

❶ My little bro, Bobby Simmons (the NBA's Most Improved Player in 2005), and my nephew, Bakari. I love them both.

❷ My thirtieth birthday with Big C. Kevin and I are both May 6 bulls, so we got together to throw a big combined bash to celebrate.

① My daughter Brittany and my son Marshawn. This was a happy night. It was Brittany's eighth grade graduation in 2001, about a year before my son was lost to me again, this time for good.

② My girls! Brittany and Peacabo, both ready to take on the world. A man couldn't hope for better daughters.

③ This little angel is my grandson, Dante, at two years old.

① Time to give back. Talking to the kids at Ready-Set-Work at the start of
stage of my life.

② Meet Rosie, one of the loves of my life. Classy, elegant, and quite the in
vidual, she captured my heart as soon as I saw her and is now part of the

On top of the world!
Testament to the power
of transformation . . .

CHAPTER ELEVEN

Coast To Coast

1986–1987 (Age 19–20 Years)

Go West Young Man

AT THE START OF MY NINETEENTH YEAR EVERYTHING WAS LOOKING ROSY. With my probation sentence completed, my time was my own again, and *party season* was in full swing.

At one of my rip-roaring house parties, I met a lady named Diane. She was a West Coast beauty from California, had come along with one of the other girls, and was having a *ball*! At one point during the evening, she ushered me to one side. She was brimming with excitement:

"Burrel, this is so *hot*! You have just *got* to bring this concept to L.A.!"

I'd been thinking about expanding the venture for some time and was keeping an eye open for suitable locations. But L.A.? Now L.A. was a whole new ball game.

"You think this'll play well in that town?"

She snorted in response, almost inhaling her drink. "*Are you kidding?*" she choked. "You'll clean up over there, Burrel."

She gestured to the partying throng behind her: "L.A.'s founded on, fuelled, and fed by this kind of stuff."

The idea began to take shape and look increasingly attractive. I'd listened often, as Tony Accardo and his cronies talked up Vegas and the City of Angels. I'd since visited Vegas many times and loved just about everything about it. But I hadn't made it as far as L.A. With things heating up in the Old Oak Brook neighborhood, now seemed a good time to look at the West Coast. I determined to expand operations and go cross-country with "Topflight Services: A Topflight Service for the Upscale."

Heading back to California as the vanguard, Diane rented a nice house, about 4,500 square feet of space, in an elegant Hollywood subdivision. This would be the nucleus of our West Coast outfit. It was a pleasant place with enough rooms for four or five live-in girls; it set us back about five thousand bucks a month.

Operations moved ahead. Diane found recruitment surprisingly easy. A number of classy, beautiful women—most with big-time acting aspirations—joined our crew. These waitresses-slash-dancers-slash-assistants-slash-beauticians-slash-actresses were waiting in the wings for their turn in the spotlight. In the meantime, they got by on L.A.'s glitzy, glossy, cosmetically enhanced stage as best they could. The opportunity we offered was a good way to make ends meet. We were in business.

> *Business is business. The man in business is strictly business. He does business and is full of business. He does not meddle in other people's business. To worry others with your business is no business. To ask the loan of a dollar is no business. To make the loan is poor business. I write this card as strictly business. Call me and see me and I will do business. If a lady loves a man, that's her business. If a man loves a lady, that's his business. Soon they are married, that's their business. If a man wishes to take a drink, that's his business. Now flip to the other side of this card, that's my business.*
>
> —Burrel's Topflight Business Card

So there we were, laid back in Los Angeles. The parties started popping, and, though operating on a less lavish scale than in Chicago, business boomed. Our West Coast setup may have been small, but it was surprisingly profitable. Folks in Hollywood were used to paying. They didn't *expect* anything for free. Just about anything you could think of could be bought and sold, and probably would be. The cash flowed as freely as the champagne.

We knew how to package a good time with style, discretion, and class. Customers poured in, and more than a few well-known faces passed through the portals of Topflight Services. Our unique setup proved to be a precursor of things to come. A few years later, in '93, Hollywood "celebrity" madam Heidi Fleiss, who lived close by in Beverly Hills, was arrested and charged with, among other things, pandering. She, it transpired, had provided services—above and beyond *massage therapy*—to some powerful and wealthy men, including Hollywood executives, actors, and world leaders. The rest, as you know, is history.

Heading South

Never a guy to think small, I saw no reason why we couldn't expand our business even further. It was time to cast the net and see what we could catch. I was *goin' fishin!*

Next stop, Miami.

I rented a wonderful house on Star Island: nearly 5,000 square feet of dazzling white-on-white, inside and out. Its pristine white days were short-lived though. I went color-crazy as soon as I got my hands on the place, transforming it into a sunshine palace, with a vibrant palette of colorful in-your-face cheeriness.

With four bedrooms, five baths, and a yacht-slip out back (in case one should be required), this was a smaller property than some of our others. It wasn't difficult to recruit beautiful women once we rolled into town, our winning formula in hand. Soon we were bursting at the seams. Still, we all squeezed in. There were girls sleeping everywhere, on beds, on sofas, even on the floor. Everyone stepped over or around everyone else, and somehow we got by.

Before long I was earning a significant revenue from the Miami setup. L.A. was growing super-fast, and Chicago, where I now had six or seven rental properties, was flourishing. I spent much of my time dashing among the three cities. I felt as though I *lived* in the hermetically sealed, twilight world of an airplane cabin.

In between trips, I juggled a fast-growing property portfolio. Development projects suited me well at this point, as they required little maintenance on my part. Once a deal was struck, I'd appoint a general contractor—a GC—to manage the job and was able to get right back to managing day-to-day business across the country.

Miami operations took off like a hot-air balloon on a breezy day. Soon we had three rental locations in full commission. I decided the time was right to make a more concrete commitment—literally—and had a large house designed and built on the beach in Clearwater. I partnered with Paul Green on this project, a friend of mine from Chicago. We put the title in his name and built a beautiful villa-style residence. More than 7,000 square feet of space, it was all cool, clean, billowing breeziness. As relaxing and private as an island hideaway, this was to be our *bachelor pad:* our place to simply lie back and chill.

Big Apple, Small Bite

New York was the next stop and would prove the toughest nut of all to crack. In my travels, I'd met a few women from that part of the world, but failed to get any bites when I floated my business proposition. One of them suggested that maybe I should look for candidates from outside the city. That gave me the idea of bringing in a team from one of our other locations.

There was no shortage of takers. The idea of taking a bite of the Big Apple was attractive, and eventually Shelly and Linda flew in from Chicago to "man" our New York outpost. Wide-eyed with excitement when they arrived, they moved into a small apartment in a smart building just across the road from Central Park.

That was my first shock. Five thousand dollars a month for a one-bedroom condo! I signed up for a short-term let, and we lived there for a while, paying rent month to month. After just eight weeks though, it was clear that the space was way too small for our requirements. We moved on to a 2,000-square-foot, three-bedroom apartment on Central Park and 45th.

This super-conservative, *bugie* building was shockingly expensive:

$12,500 a month. And *man* did that place get hot fast! The block was full of old dears who'd lived there since the foundations went down, back in the thirties. Everyone knew everyone else's business, and it was soon made crystal clear that we, most definitely, *were not* welcome. In the four months that we rented there, I entered the place no more than six times.

New York was hard to break into on all fronts. We began working the clubs, greasing palms wherever we went, and spreading the word that we were in business. For the most part, our message fell on deaf ears and growth was slow. We were successful in attracting new girls though. Once Shelly and Linda got out and about, word got around. We took calls from plenty of women who wanted to join us. Still it took a full six months to build up to a crew of ten, and for most of the time we operated in New York, five women carried the business.

And man, those New York guys were *hardcore!*

A *hit* in the ultraconservative Midwest, we were *adored* in free-wheeling, sexy L.A., and guys just *threw* themselves at us in sun-kissed Miami. But, New York? Forget it! There was no way these dudes were going to put their hands in their pockets for anything other than a little *pocket pool.* New York guys apparently thought the girls should be paying *them* for the privilege of their company.

Still crack it we did, though on a relatively small scale. Once we were ten strong, my income was substantial, although most of it was eaten up, straight away, by outrageously high overheads. Trust me, New York is *no* place for the fainthearted.

Growing Pains

I checked out Atlanta next. This was one town where it was clear, from the moment I got off the plane, that *nothing* was going down. The few lucrative spots—the casinos and big clubs—were already sewn up tighter than drums. More damning from my perspective, though, was that the locals I ran into, seemed happy with what little was already on offer in that good town, and a lap dance was about as *risqué* as they were likely to get. Nope, conservative Atlanta didn't look good for me. I quickly moved on.

The last port of call was San Francisco. I didn't actually spend time myself in that city, but sent a scout ahead to reconnoiter. We rented a small apartment and put some feelers out, but before too long, Janine returned to the fold in L.A. San Fran was a no-go.

Back in L.A., we were becoming better organized. With a couple of locations in full swing, we'd become wise to the value of "marketing" and were experimenting with ads in the yellow pages. With this more mainstream approach to promotion came additional problems and care had to be taken to filter calls. Previously, customers had been acquired by word-of-mouth recommendation only. Now anyone could call, anytime. For the girls' security, we had to make sure our customers were legitimate and traceable. Apart from concerns about the well-being of the women, any stranger could easily be an undercover cop ferreting around.

The majority of our clients continued to arrive through personal referrals though, and by running our business from privately rented addresses, we protected ourselves, to the greatest extent possible, from the attentions of the law.

Undercover guys in the clubs and bars would shake the girls down at the drop of a hat. High-class bars, clubs, and luxury hotels—even places that charged three and four hundred bucks a night—were regularly staked out, and raided. There wasn't a lot anyone could do though, about an exclusive massage service, operating out of an elegant residential address.

Chicago, Miami, New York, and L.A. were locked down by my twentieth birthday. More than 360 girls, across four states, worked with Topflight. More than three hundred of whom chose to stay with the organization for over a year and a half. During this golden period, we took in between $300,000 and $400,000 a day.

Back in Florida, my partner Paul and I partied in the Clearwater house as if every day was to be our last. Trouble was brewing though. Paul had started messing around with a few of the girls, playing one off against the other. It was a situation that was causing friction and had to be handled.

I didn't want to fall out with Paul. I needed him. He was an important financial partner and *conduit*. I'd give him hard cash to buy whatever needed to be bought, and being a guy with that winning combination of good credit and extraordinary financial acumen, he'd finesse the payments through legal channels. Everything was in his name—the house we built, the cars, and all the rental properties. He was, in effect, my banker.

I managed all my business dealings in this manner. Over the years, I worked with six or seven trusted friends who conducted my fiscal transactions. I'd give them the cash, plus profit, and they'd structure the financing. I'd hold the titles or deeds in order to make sure payment had been made and the car/house/furniture wouldn't be repossessed the next day. The whole process might take up to six months, but at the end of the day, my name wasn't directly associated with any assets.

Successfully navigating these early glitches in an otherwise smooth relationship, Paul and I stayed tight. Unfortunately, it was an indicator of future friction, and in time Paul and I would fall out more seriously. Our squabbles weren't the only worrying portent either. I was doing so well I got overconfident, and began gambling on a large scale—not at the gaming tables but in the stock market.

King-Sized Gambling Habits

After my catastrophic $10 million dice roll a couple of years earlier, I'd stood back from gaming. I watched Wenny, with increasing incomprehension, as he squandered *huge* sums of money at the dice table. I joined him on a few occasions, in a throw or two, but afterwards always felt like a fool. No, I'd decided long ago, gambling wasn't for me, so when I *did* succumb to its temptations, I didn't even recognize it for what it was. I just called it *stock trading*.

My buddy Dee had a couple of friends who had a seat at the New York Stock Exchange. Since I was working with large amounts of capital, Joe and Mike were keen to meet up with me. We got together early in 1987, and they put a *cold* offer on the table. Joe proposed that we work together, trade my funds through second-party accounts, and clean the cash using the stock market as our laundry. It was going to cost me 25 percent of my capital. To offset that zinger, they promised that the trades we'd make would be winners. We'd work the market and cream off big profits. It was all too tempting.

We started with a $50,000 test run. Dee called me after four days. He sounded a bit down: "We din' do too good, bro,'" he drawled. "But I'll go ahead and split it anyway, like we promised. You still got your share comin'."

Sure enough, he showed up later that day and handed me papers that showed my $50,000 stake was now worth $72,000! Four days, no work, and a $22,000 *squeaky-clean* profit? Damn, I was hooked! Problem was, of course, I was hooked on a *mirage*. I was richer only on paper, but that was a lesson I wouldn't absorb until much later.

In the meantime, I set up an account—all cash, of course—with Joe and Mike's brokerage, and we started moving large amounts of money through the system. They had some major players on their books and would simply blend my trades into the broader swathe of transactions they handled each day. They'd slide out our profits and reinvest them into more stock. My nose was open, *wide open!*

I found myself pouring in more money every day. Buying large blocks of predominantly high-tech shares, I'd trade $10,000 and $20,000 at a time. It was a volatile period for the economy, and the market fluctuated wildly. In reality, it was nothing more than a craps shoot. But some days, I was Midas himself. With the size of my holdings, the profit and loss potential was enormous. When I made money, I made lots. This reduced the impact of those days I fared less well, and over time I sort of lost track of whether I was up or down at any given moment.

Then something happened, traumatic enough, to push this and all the other day-to-day stuff *right* out of my head.

CHAPTER TWELVE

Betrayal

1987 (Age 20 Years)

Wenny: Act III

BACK IN CHICAGO, REILLY GAVE ME THE HEADS UP THAT TROUBLE WAS BREWING. He'd been given a tip-off that Wenny was *sizzling* and about to go down. He warned me to stay clear of him. This wasn't going to be a problem. Wiz and I weren't kickin' it much these days, after a nasty falling out a few weeks earlier.

Gambling more extravagantly than ever, Wenny had the habit *real bad* now and spent almost every day and night in the gambling dens, trying to find some sucker willing to take him on.

An accomplished cheat, he was invincible when playing with his own loaded deck or dice. But these days, his reputation usually preceded him, and pickings were slim. He was losing more often than he won, but like all addicts, couldn't wait for the next roll of the dice so he could win it all back. One rainy night he turned up the house at Nacoma Drive on the hunt for funds.

By now, I'd poured nearly $4 million back into the ghetto. Wenny had taken well over $2 million in *loans*, money we both knew would never be collected, and the rest had been parceled out to the dozens of guys I knew, who were just treading water out there.

There are always hands reaching out to you from the ghetto. Guys who need a few bucks seed money for a new business, or bond money, or funds to hire a lawyer, or a few dollars to pay the rent. That's the ghetto, though, clawing back whatever's been taken out. It has a case that's hard to argue with, and you'd have to be pretty callous to turn your back on debts owed and relationships forged. In the months since I'd departed, I'd been paying with interest.

> *During the last two years, I've been trying to get out. But once in the racket, you're always in it, it seems. The parasites trail you, begging you for favors and for money, and you can never get away from them, no matter where you go.*[18]
>
> —Al Capone

But Wiz was a different story. He just kept coming back, seemed to feel that I owed him. I knew he still claimed credit for my successes, even though I'd long since gone my own way. I harbored a strong suspicion, too, that Wenny had his own stash of cash. Just like the old days, when we'd preferred to use my dad's money rather than our own, Wiz didn't plan on using his own resources to fund his habits.

I understood this, but the first few times he came a-calling I thought, *"Ah, what the heck. I'll go and hit him with it. We're both guys out of the same game"* and I'd pay up.

At the same time though, I tried to show him an alternative way. I talked to him about what I was up to; the real estate and property deals I was doing; the businesses I'd set up and how swell it all was. Wiz paid attention. He'd listen hard, make all the right noises, beat his chest a little, and at the end of our talk would pledge to *wise up* and change his ways.

And, of course, it was all so much *bullshit*. Just a short-term (and

---

18. Capone quote taken from Gus Russo's *The Outfit* (Bloomsbury, 2003), and was apparently uttered during a conversation between Capone and a Philadelphia public safety director, while Capone was (allegedly on his own initiative) incarcerated in late 1929 and early 1930.

short-sighted) strategy to keep me happy long enough for him to get his hands on some more of my cash. Eventually, I had to call it quits with Wiz.

So when he showed up around two in the morning, it didn't take a super-sleuth to know he didn't have socializing on his mind. Right enough. He was in the door less than a minute and was already down to business.

"Hey, bro. Hit me with a coupla hun'red G."

I was wearing a robe and pajamas, eyes squinty with sleep. "*Hell no,* man. I don' have it."

He was piqued and, apparently, *incredulous.* His characteristic charm held—though clearly strained. "Don' give me that *shit,* man. I *know* you got it. I know that *ain't nuthin'* to you."

"Not to put back in the game, Wiz." I stood my ground. "I ain't throwing no more back to the streets."

After thirty minutes of verbal fisticuffs and emotional blackmail, I relented, pulling $50,000 from a kitchen drawer.

I handed it to him. "Here you go, bro. Best I can do."

He took the money, looked at it as if it were contaminated, looked at me as if I were too, and in total fury *flung* the whole lot back in my face.

"Don' you give me no fuckin' fifty G, you cheap ass *nigga!*" His face was mottled with anger. "Tha's what you give a bitch to have her a shopping trip, *nigga!*"

With that Wenny swung around and stormed out of the house.

I'd see him at a distance over the following weeks, but with so many demands on my time and my tough travel schedule, we didn't run into each other the way we used to.

Night Crawlers

So the warning call from Reilly didn't really alarm me. After Wiz and I fought, I'd had a niggling concern that maybe I should move my money from under the kitchen floor. But frankly, it was locked down so tight, it seemed like a lot of trouble for probably no good cause. At the end of the day, Wiz was doing his thing and I was doing mine. We may have fallen out, but we were still brothers. There was no way that Wiz would betray me. Our history, our relationship, and the bonds of brotherhood ran far too deep.

This particular night I'd just arrived home from an extended multi-city trip. It was after midnight, and I was exhausted. Conditioned my entire life to be nocturnal—in my world that was usually when the action went down—I was already acclimatized to upside-down days. I'd frequently stay up all night, sometimes for several on end, and catch my sleep in snatches during the day. I usually averaged only three or four hours of rest, out of every twenty-four, and some weeks I felt as though I hadn't seen more than a glimmer of daylight.

I adopted a favorite live music joint in each city, where I liked to hang out and chill. In Miami, it was an exuberant little salsa bar; in L.A., I preferred the lobby bar at the Four Seasons; in Chicago, I usually ended up at this cool reggae club called the Wild House. My usual, fail-safe routine for unwinding involved sitting and smoking, until the small hours, sipping a cocktail or two, listening to the music, and, if in the mood, dancing until I wore myself out.

But tonight I was already worn out. I'd been on the go for weeks, my mind careening in all directions, 24/7. I was both physically and emotionally drained. Tonight there was nothing on my mind, but a Jacuzzi, followed by a great movie, and then that *sweet* California king bed!

After soaking in the huge tub, I wrapped myself in my favorite silk paisley robe and put on one of my favorite movies: *Casablanca*. Lounging with my feet propped up, I quietly smoked my last joint. It was rare for me to run out of weed, but somehow I'd miscalculated and had failed to top up my supply; I was smoking this baby slowly and *appreciatively*.

I was in the habit of drinking gallons of water while I relaxed, and tonight was no exception. I had a bottle in hand, and a couple of empties lay on the floor. Before long I *needed* to take a piss. I went to the bathroom and, while I was at it, took a last hit on my joint, threw the duck down the toilet, and flushed.

I went back to watching *Casablanca*, but soon *Casablanca* was *watching me*. I was dead to the world.

I couldn't have asleep more than fifteen or twenty minutes—the movie was still running when I opened my eyes—before *all hell* broke loose. I was yanked out of my dreams by an ear-splitting *BOOM* reverberating from the front of the house, followed by a *massive* crash. I popped up like toast, eyes wide with shock, but already it was over.

My bedroom was full of cops; black clad, pistol-toting, body-armored cops. Surrounding the bed, flashlights full in my face, they appeared supernaturally huge. Beams of light jumped around the room, strobe-like, chasing the shadows and each other up the walls and crawling across the ceiling. Partially blinded by the light, it took me a moment to focus and a few more to gather my wits.

Someone clicked a switch and artificial, electric brightness flooded the room with shocking suddenness, transforming it into the vividly lit set of a horror movie. Men in black crowded around the bed pushing their guns right in my face.

One of them hissed at me, "You're Burrel Wilks Junior, and we're gonna *take a ride*."

As a man who'd experienced many unpleasant surprises in his life, I was mentally conditioned to cope with pretty much any curve ball thrown at me. But *this* was a mind-jarring nightmare that no previous experience could have prepared me for. Even today, I hear the echo of my front door caving in, and those heavy boots on the stairs.

My privacy violated in the most ugly manner, it would be years before I'd recapture the sense of security a firmly locked front door had once allowed me—and enjoy another worry-free night's sleep.

The cops dragged me out of bed and read me my rights. Refusing to let me take my trousers and shirt from the clothes stand in the corner of the room, they flung my robe at me then frog-marched me down the stairs to one of the waiting cars. We headed, in convoy, down to the precinct station. I was pulled out of the car and unceremoniously propelled into a holding cell.

This was the last time I was to set foot in my dream home in Old Oak Brook. If the neighbors had been hoping for divine intervention, they got it, though I suspect it was louder and better-armed than even they'd bargained for!

The Great Setback

I spent four days in the police cells before being extricated by Reilly, my lawyer. The narcotics squad looked hard—real hard—for evidence of drugs. They'd torn the place apart but found no illegal substances, not even a joint. Thank heaven my last blunt was swirling its way through the sewer system long before the morning peace was shattered by thundering footfalls.

And, of course, there weren't any narcotics to be found. I was out of the game, and all their intelligence would have confirmed that. What they were really after was the fortune under the floor. They knew it was there. Wenny had done his job well, selling me out in exchange for his own freedom. Tiles were smashed and floors were ripped up as they dug deep and hauled out the boxes of cash. My *going-nowhere* money headed south.

It was a no-win situation. In classic street-style, I'd been super-clever in cleaning up my cash but not quite smart enough covering my tracks. The cloak of legitimacy I'd cast around myself wasn't thick enough to divert anyone for more than a moment. My official income simply couldn't account for buried reserves of this magnitude. The cops told me that I was *"some kind of Teflon muthafucka."* They'd been trying to pin me down for years. Everyone knew of Buddy Burrel, but there had never been anything tangible to grab onto, until now. I'd always slipped through the net.

There were a number of good reasons for this. I was shrewd enough to keep moving. I stayed away from ghetto *black holes*, had numerous residential addresses, was a loner, and was careful in how I moved my cash around. My *patois-patter* and Jamaican persona threw everyone for a loop, too.

Even now, they didn't have a direct case against me. The house deeds were in the name of a girlfriend's father, and the cars had been purchased through my uncle's good credit. Both men cracked under the pressure of questioning and told the Feds that I'd given them the cash to make the necessary transactions. Although I was upset with them at the time, looking back I can't blame them. I'm not sure they had any other option—the money trail had to lead somewhere, and there was no place for it to go, except to me.

Reilly struck a deal on my behalf. No direct charges would be brought against me—it's unlikely they would have stuck in any case—but everything that had been seized would be forfeit. On day four of my incarceration, I was informed that my house and its contents, including the cash and cars, were to be confiscated by the government. I couldn't argue. They weren't officially mine in any case.

So I lost it all, my dream home, "party-central," my stable of beautiful automobiles, and *vast* amounts of cash. The financial loss was huge, the emotional blow stunning, and the betrayal *colossal*.

Wenny was my brother, but he sold me out *without blinking*.

How can I explain?

You grow up with a guy. You're closer than fingers in a fist. You run together, break bread, party and play, work and dream. Sometimes you fight, too, but more often you laugh. You spend days, months, and years at each other's side; your family becomes *his*; you and he are *brothers* in everything but blood. Even though, on an intellectual level, you *know* his potential for faithlessness, you believe the bonds of your shared past will be stronger than self-interest. The blow, the day you find out you're wrong, is *crushing*.

Ghetto telegraphs were singing across the city. Everyone thought it was all over for the King. Burrel was washed up and out of the game. *Not a chance.*

Family Plots

I'd been moving paper around the country for some time now. Pockets of it were salted away all over the place; tied up in property, real estate projects, and stocks and shares or just tucked away in corners. Possibly the most unlikely cache, though, was the several million bucks buried deep in my *own grave*.

I'd bought some parcels of land years earlier in a North Side cemetery overlooking the skating rink on Lawrence. Death is never far from anyone's mind in the ghetto, and initially I'd bought the plot—together with a nice little tombstone—as a contingency in the event of my untimely end. Not required yet for its primary purpose, I soon saw more immediate potential for my hole in the ground. It would make a first-rate, if somewhat unusual, *safety deposit box*.

Befriending the cemetery superintendent, an older guy and ex-Vice Lord, I slid him in on the scheme. This was necessary. I had to make sure that my plot would never be relocated, something that happens in some cemeteries as overpopulation stretches them to bursting point. We had a serious chat, made our arrangements, and he dutifully turned a blind eye. Like my dad before me, I became a kind of "grave robber" in reverse.

Instead of plundering this grave, I snuck in at night, dug deep, and packed it with sacks of cash.

So even after the Old Oak Brook debacle, even though emotionally battered, I was still afloat financially. My net worth—on paper at least—was healthy. I was liquid and had a good income stream, and although losing the Chicago party HQ set me back some, I remained a *playa* to be reckoned with.

Spiraling Overheads

Unfortunately, my fiscal sense didn't increase in inverse proportion to the sharp decline in my fortune.

I continued to plow money back into the ghetto, jumping from one get-quick-rich scheme to another: $20,000 here, $50,000 there. I was the behind-the-scenes "angel investor" for a lot of guys I'd grown up around, their friends, friends-of-their-friends, and anyone else who brought a good idea my way. Once word got around, if someone didn't know me before, they soon made sure they did.

It was important to me to show the world that I hadn't failed, that I was still a man of means. I can probably name upwards of forty little Mom-and-Pop ventures that I helped fund—part of the great-gray-ghetto economy. Beauty salons, restaurants, car washes, barbershops, fashion retailers, and barbeque businesses flourished, floundered, or failed. You name it, I probably had money in it. Now I don't care how wealthy you are, this kind of stuff is guaranteed to nibble *any* fortune to death.

I continued buying and selling property and developing everything from strip malls to apartment blocks. I made money on most and lost my shirt on some. And income continued to flow in through Topflight Services—around a quarter of a million on a good day—adding up to between $4 million or $5 million monthly. Most was plowed straight back into the business, sucked up as overhead.

The costs of running Topflight had escalated tremendously. We had the houses to maintain, of course, as well as the cost of running the cars and living expenses. We also paid for security, masseurs, manicurists, hairdressers, pool guys, gardeners, dental and medical care, and a myriad of other services. Then there were the parties! We didn't skimp on anything; the food, wine, flowers, and entertainment were lavish. My bills regularly added up to between $400,000 and $500,000 weekly.

My friends at the brokerage, in the meantime, continued to fleece me. As well as siphoning off the agreed 25 percent in fees, they took commissions on all my other trades. The rewards still seemed to outweigh the price, however, and I kept salting funds away in the form of stocks and currency, convinced that this was to be my retirement plan. Joe and Mike knew how to work it, all right. They lined up a whole gang of different channels through which to work my numbers *for* me and, ultimately, *on* me. I was paying close to 50 percent off the top of all transactions, and the stocks my funds found their way into were highly volatile.

And that was my problem, of course: everything I did, I *overdid.* I'd been this way ever since I was a little kid. A man of extremes, I never learned how to do *anything* in moderation. My passion, enthusiasm, energy, and loyalty were all extreme, as were my dreams, aspirations, and, unfortunately, my cash flow!

Clothesaholic

Clothes don't make a man, they say. True, but the manner in which you *package* yourself is essential to how positively you are perceived. The art of self-branding is something I've intuitively understood my whole life. Fine clothes are a great pleasure, but also a practical work tool.

Wenny introduced me to street-sharp style when I was just a *shorty,* and my appetite for superior tailoring was further whetted during those basement meetings at Tony's house. But credit for my transformation from *ghetto-chic* to *style-guru* goes to a great friend, Big John. He taught me that classy, classic clothes were a *passport* that could take me anywhere in the world.

"Burrel, wearin' what you wearin' you can go anywhere on the West Side," he'd say, "but a nigga like you gotta go *global,* man!"

I still sported my "fatigue-front" when appropriate, but I wasn't wed to them now that they'd served their purpose. I cultivated *expensive* shopping habits. As in so many other areas of my life, I was compulsive and just a little excessive! A well-known face on Chicago's Magnificent Mile, L.A.'s Rodeo Drive, Fifth Avenue in New York, and South Beach in Florida,

I'd spend between twenty and twenty-five G's in any given week on clothes, depending on what caught my eye.

Prada, Gucci, Brioni, and Boss. Armani, Ambugli, Versace, and Zegna. I bought them by the armful. Silk ties; handcrafted leather shoes, belts, and bags; mink, leather, suede, finely spun wool, cashmere, and linen. You name it—*I had to have it!*

Was I vain? You *bet*! Some nights, sauntering into a restaurant or club, I'd be so intent on catching a glimpse of my reflection that I'd all but *trip* over my finely clad feet, or walk into a mirror, or through a closed door. I thought I looked as sharp as a double-edged razor.

There were plenty of opportunities to shine, too. Almost every night, I ate out at fine and fancy restaurants—usually in the company of fine and fancy women. I frequented exclusive clubs and drank champagne in *who's-who* watering holes. I was in my element.

CHAPTER THIRTEEN

Golfing With God

Godfather

GODFATHER WAS ACTUALLY CHRISTENED BURRELL. Burrell Henry wasn't related to the Wilkses by blood, but because of the closeness of our first names, people assumed he was. It was a name that was always mixed up in one scandal or another. We *heard* of Burrell long before we actually *met* him.

Godfather was from Columbus, Georgia, and to hear him tell the story, he left the state in order to avoid serving time on a chain gang. The first time he fell foul of the law was at the tender age of four. One of nine boys and five girls, they each learned to hustle just to get by. His older brothers had a nice piece of action going: they robbed the local schoolhouse with almost predictable regularity.

The technique was quite simple and streamlined through practice. Young Burrell, just a scrap of a boy at the time, would be suspended on a rope and lowered down the chimney. He'd rifle the room, grab what he could, and let himself out the front door, whereupon his brothers would usually beat him around the head and extract the spoils. This went on for years. It worked well, too—until the day he was *caught*.

After this first recorded misdemeanor, Burrell Henry couldn't seem to stay out of trouble. In and out of various homes for delinquent boys, he became a familiar face to authorities. By his nineteenth year, he was staring hard time straight in the eye.

Shouldering his backpack, he hooked up with his cousin Tommy, and the two of them skipped town. Setting off for Chicago, they kept one wary eye over their shoulders all the way. With not a dime to their names, they hitched and hiked north. Stealing chickens and eggs (and on one lucky occasion, a pig), grilling sparrows and songbirds on spits; foraging for vegetables and fungi; begging, gambling, and sleeping in barns, they tramped, meandered, odd-jobbed, and scavenged their way across more than eight hundred miles.

Tommy peeled off in Indiana, and after parting company with him, Burrell Henry continued on alone to Chicago. He arrived in the city in 1963, just a year or so before my dad. The city was a colossal, bustling metropolis the likes of which this Georgia small-town boy had *never* seen.

But Burrell Henry wasn't intimidated, and didn't plan on dragging his feet. In only a matter of days, he successfully established himself as a force in the neighborhood. Those first few days in the city, he'd been sleeping on the second floor of his uncle's house, spending hours at the window, scanning the street below. The lay of the land seemed clear: each night, the same local *tough* hustled the same street corner dealing, dicing, and apparently making out pretty good.

Burrell Henry did fifty push-ups, went downstairs, crossed the road, and without a word—in front of at least fifteen witnesses—knocked the guy out cold! Burrell was built. A burly, bluff boy with a full beard, a shaved head, and a drawl that was distinctly Georgia, he claimed, improbably, to hail from the West Coast. *No one* was about to argue with him, and folks soon took to calling him "California."

A week or two later, California had hooked up with a couple of girls and turned his hand to pimping. This would be his "trade" for years to come. Eventually, he built up a small team of three or four girls, all with the distinctive trademark of a shaved head just like his own. Despite his quirky appearance, California had a reputation for ruthlessly keeping his girls in line.

He made enough money—probably on average four or five grand each day—to pay for a good style of living. But money had a tendency to trickle through his fingers, never pausing long enough to visit his pockets along the way. He spent the stuff as fast as he made it. He shopped, smoked, and splurged and whatever was left got taken to the craps tables, where it could easily be doubled—or lost. Oh yes, California loved to gamble and was an accomplished player—especially when the dice were loaded in his favor.

Soon *California* morphed into *The President* then into *King Burrell* and eventually into *Godfather.* This handle stuck, and as Godfather, Burrell Henry became one of the most flamboyant and recognizable pimps in Chicago.

He marked out his territory on Halstead, adopting a simple but effective strategy to reduce competitive pressure: he took pot shots at the other pimps from a nearby railway bridge with an R30 rifle. As a deterrent, it's fair to say it worked *damn well.* Faster than a Times Square pickpocket, the corner emptied and Godfather's business took off.

If you play with fire, expect to get *burned.* Just before he turned twenty-one, Godfather had the first of many brushes with death. He'd been messing with a local girl and one night dumped her publicly. Humiliated and angry, she reported to her father that Burrell had beaten her. Her father, known for his protectiveness, came *a-lookin'* for Godfather.

Now Burrell was no angel, and he had been known to lay hands on women, but it so happened that this time he was innocent. When the girl's father turned up for a showdown, Godfather willingly followed him outside to talk. But there was to be no talking. Papa Williams shot Godfather three times, at point blank range. Burrell lay on the freezing ground while people clustered around him, pressing snow into his wounds to slow the bleeding. He survived, but in his lifetime—to date—would be shot a total of *thirteen* times. And those were only the bullets that found their mark.

Rocks and Flowers—All Pink and Purple

Since as early as the 1850s, Chicago pimps have adopted a flamboyant, diamond-encrusted code of dress. It's their way of advertising, the equivalent of handing out a business card or a brochure. Like many other pimps, Godfather reveled in the outrageous.

He wore *only* pink and purple: pink on one side and purple on the other. His suits were two-toned, flowery affairs, tailored at great expense to fit impeccably. Paired with equally mismatched dress shoes, the whole ensemble was brought together with a wide brimmed hat and huge plastic-rimmed shades. Godfather's uniforms, his bushy beard, and his hard-boiled countenance painted him as something of a character, but you underestimated him at your own risk.

Godfather lived in a pink and purple house on Center Street in Harvey, Illinois. He had a custom pink and purple Rolls Royce Silver Shadow and used to collect *rocks*. Yup, rocks. He invested a fortune over the years—literally hundreds of thousands of dollars—on *tons* of everyday rocks, which for some unfathomable reason pleased him aesthetically. He'd have them shipped to his front garden and, once they were strategically positioned, would paint them—pink and purple.

I remember one incident that still leaves me laughing every time I think about it. Godfather had purchased a rock—a *large* rock—and had to somehow get it to his house. We went to pay for it (more than two thousand bucks!), and the guy who'd sold it, a builder, offered to deliver it for another couple of hundred. Godfather paced around the huge hunk, scratching his beard and sizing it up. The damn thing seemed as big as the Sears Tower! It must have weighed in at more than a ton, but still Godfather decided he wasn't prepared to shell out any more money. Self-delivery was *clearly* the solution.

With the help of heavy equipment, the great lump of stone was man-handled into Godfather's rusty old van, a red Chevy. The whole structure groaned, sighed, and sagged with the effort. All four tires flat to the road, we started limping for home—making it precisely four hundred yards before the entire infrastructure collapsed under the terrible load. Axles contorting in all directions, the undercarriage hit pavement with the dreadful squeal of giant fingernails across an enormous blackboard. The truck was a *write-off*! A tow vehicle had to be brought in to shift the debris, and Godfather still had to pay the extra two hundred bucks to get that damn rock home!

Godfather loved other kinds of "rocks" as well—the (more) expensive, glittery ones. He was finally forced to shorten his handle from *Godfather* to *God* when he found out just how much it cost to emboss his full name, in diamonds, on a bracelet.

God's pink and purple house became somewhat famous during the seventies and eighties, and was a regular stopping point for tourist buses until the night, in the late eighties, when it was vaporized by a lightning strike. Everything God owned went up in smoke though he, fortunately, was out. He still tells the tale of how he felt an inexplicable itch to go to town that night, even though it was the wrong side of midnight and a storm was brewing. He hit town, lightning hit his house, and the rest is history. Whatever caused that itch, scratching it almost certainly saved his life.

L.A. Requiem

Buoyed by his financial success in Chicago, God decided to take his show on the road. The West Coast had been tugging at him like a kid on his coattails, and at twenty-nine years of age, he loaded up the Rolls and set out for L.A. God reckoned if he could make money with his working girls, their asses *freezing off* in the Windy City, then it stood to reason he could make a *killin'* in L.A. He was off to play that warm weather game!

With $25,000 tucked into the trunk of the double-R, he set off on the 2,000-plus-mile trip, taking his time, keeping within the speed limit, and savoring the journey. Arriving in Hollywood a week or so later, everything was as it *should* be.

Damn, L.A. looked good! The women were stunning: all sun-kissed hair, tanned skin, long legs, and white, white smiles. Oh, yes, it was going to be a *pleasure* taking over this town! Dressed in his finest threads, God took up position on the corner of Sunset Strip and Hollywood Boulevard, a more upmarket *stroll* than he was used to. He cast out his net with anticipation.

It came in empty. Worse, he was just about laughed off the block. At the sight of God, pimps and prostitutes alike all but wept with laughter. In the early seventies, the dress code adopted by pimps on the West Coast was, well, *seventies*. Blue jeans were prevalent, and although there was more than a little flash trash around, no one came *close* to God's flowery flamboyance.

The Californians nicknamed this Huggy Bear apparition in the pink and purple suit and matching fedora, *Flowers*. God had expected many reactions from L.A., but ridicule wasn't one of them. Furious and humiliated though he was, he was also one thickheaded man. God wasn't budging.

After he'd hung around for few more fruitless weeks, a well-meaning prostitute took him to the side and advised him to lose the suit, the hat, the shoes, and *the car*. God was outraged.

"Is you *crazy*, bitch? That car cost mo' than yo' sorry ass'll earn in this lifetime! Tha' car ain't going *nowhere!*"

Three weeks later, Godfather was back in Chi-town with $2,000 in his pocket and his tail between his legs. *To hell* with California!

The Bishop and Mr. T

During his late twenties, Godfather had become friendly with another infamous Chicago pimp, Bishop Don "Magic" Juan.[19] Bishop a.k.a. Donald Campbell was younger than Godfather. He'd recently come home from the service, liked Burrell's style, and became keen to make his own mark in the world of pimping. The two had much in common and friendship developed.

Sharing an affinity with God for, among other things, flashy attire, Bishop was, and is to this day, a green and gold kind of guy. He liked to sport rhinestone-encrusted green suits, thickly embossed with heavy gold embroidery. Eventually, rhinestones were replaced with diamonds, but for the time being, glitz was enough. Always seen carrying a heavily be-jeweled staff, Bishop cut quite a dash.

If his outfits didn't get him noticed, then his bodyguard would. For years, Bishop didn't go anywhere without Mr. T at his side. Mr. T hailed from the notorious Cabrini Green Projects, was built like an oil tanker, and wore enough gold to feed a small country for a few years. Prior to his entry onto both the large and small screen, he made a career out of body-guarding and bouncing. He became a celebrity of some stature after being discovered by Sylvester Stallone and appearing in *Rocky III* and a number of other productions (notably the television show *The A-Team*). For years though, Godfather, Bishop, and Mr. T were familiar figures around Chicago, along with Godfather's brother Lewis Henry a.k.a. Messiah.

---

19. *From Pimp Stick to Pulpit—It's Magic: The Life Story of Don "Magic" Juan*, Ann Bromfield, Bishop Don Juan, and Katheryn L. Patterson (Vantage Press, 1994).

Bishop and Godfather were founders of the Four Aces Club, a sort of "pimps' social society." God was the Spade, Bishop the Diamond, General the Heart, and Cadillac the Club—pimps all. They even opened up a clubhouse, a place for players to let their hair down, gamble, play pool, and just let rip. It wasn't unusual to see huddles of pimps, flanked by their flashy cars, congregating on Madison and just chillin'. I guess even pimps need *family*.

By the time Godfather returned from L.A. with his empty pockets and dented ego, his girls had jumped ship. God scaled down operations, and for the next twenty years or so, his only working prostitute, and companion, was a woman named Angela.

Even though he was never more than small-time, more often than not, God managed to land in the thick of any trouble that was going around. As late as 2002, he narrowly escaped death when out and about in Chicago, with Bishop Don Juan, King Boo, and Doc. They were sitting at the traffic lights in Boo's gold Mercedes, when four men surrounded the vehicle and opened fire at point blank range.

Boo, an old and good personal friend, was probably the target. He died instantly. Bishop, sitting in the passenger seat, *miraculously* escaped being hit, although his white mink coat was riddled with enough holes to look like Swiss cheese. Doc, sitting just behind Boo, was injured. God survived without a scratch.

Golfer-On-Duty (G.O.D.)

God's real passion was gambling, and when not at the craps table, the best way he knew to make money was by playing golf. He was an *extraordinary*, spectacularly talented trick golfer and could make just about any shot you could conceive and some you never would. He had a whole repertoire of jaw-dropping moves: a three-hundred-yard drive taken from his knees, or with one hand, while sitting on the little folding chair he always carried around. He could take a putter and hit the ball two hundred yards off a tee or sink a golf ball from two hundred feet with a seven iron. That man could make balls curl around corners. I mean he was phenomenal!

I'd met God when I was a *shorty*. We'd taken a shine to each other and knocked around now and again, but recently, he'd been spending more time with me, teaching me the basics of golf. I decided to make it official and hire him as my teacher. For the next few years, I paid him several thousand bucks a week for intensive lessons. I was getting serious about this game, and it was getting serious about me!

This man and I had a special relationship. After my dad had hit the skids and I'd broken away from him, I began hanging out more frequently with Godfather. As Topflight Services expanded countrywide and flourished financially, God's fortunes waned. It seemed as though we could help each other out. He became my teacher, my driver, and my right-hand man. We had stuff to do everywhere, places to be. Whenever I could get away, we'd crisscross the country by car, playing golf along the way.

God was the most unlikely looking golfing genius you could imagine. After his house had gone up in flames, taking most of his pink and purple attire with it, he evolved his wardrobe to include suits made up to look like decks of cards and custom jackets with G.O.D.—Golfer On Duty—embossed on the back. He'd turn up at a clubhouse in his mismatched, in-your-face uniforms, and inevitably some zealous club official would try to block his entrance.

"You can't enter dressed like that, sir, I'm afraid," he'd stutter. "We have a dress code here, you know."

"Well, so do I," God would say. "An' *this* is my code."

"But, sir, you aren't even wearing the right shoes. You need spikes," the hapless club employee would continue.

"*Man,* them spikes leave holes in the grass! Now mine, they's *smooth*!"

The argument usually went the same way. The official would explain that flat soles could cut up the green when your feet twisted. God would insist on demonstrating that his feet *never* twisted, and would effortlessly make a three-hundred-yard shot. As soon as the officials saw how he played, the gates to the Forbidden Kingdom swung open magically.

Striding onto the course, gold chains and diamonds tinkling like wind chimes, you'd hear us coming a mile off. We were just as noisy visually. God had an innovative golf bag, made out of a saucepan and several slim steel rods. The contraption looked like a mobile umbrella stand with see-through sides. Wheeling this miraculous invention around the course, whenever he stopped to take a shot, he'd nonchalantly stand it upright and stabilize the whole contrivance by spearing the spike attached to its base into the grass.

One day we were queuing up to pay green fees at an exclusive golf course in Florida, and a bluff, red-faced, middle-aged man, who was standing just behind us, took one look at God's jacket and started sniggering. "*GOD!*" he snorted derisively. "I wouldn't call *him* God!"

Godfather spun around and looked him cold in the eye: "You just did, *muthafucka*. You just did."

God took a fortune from the pockets of a long list of complacent men who couldn't reconcile the image of the man in the joker suit, with the notion of being trounced on the green. More often than not, they left the game confidence *shaken* and stereotypes *stirred*. Unsuspecting doctors, dentists, politicians, and businessmen fell in swathes, for the most part speechless, on occasion furious, but always with lighter wallets. We were making thousands of dollars each week, doing what we loved best.

Ironically, God dispatched these deadly *stealth* attacks from the loudest of launch pads, invisible but in plain sight. *No one* could miss him coming, yet somehow, they usually *did*.

Limos and Diamonds

One night, after a strenuous day on the golf course, I had a dream. In this dream, I was driving a white stretch limo and sporting a five-carat diamond in my nose. When I woke, and blinked the sleep from my eyes and mind, it was clear this wasn't a portent to be ignored. I wasn't sure what path it would steer me down, but I intended to follow the signposts. I went straight out and bought a white, ten-passenger stretch.

I already possessed the perfect five-carat gem in the form of an ear-stud. I had it reset and went down to the local beauty salon to get my nose pierced. It didn't look like the kind of place that did too many noses. Their piercing machine was an old staple gun that sounded like a twenty-two caliber pistol, and possibly *felt* like one, too. The damn thing jammed twice during what turned out to be an *excruciatingly* painful procedure. I emerged shaken, but with the prerequisite hole in my nose. Instructed to wait at least two months before swapping the surgical stud for anything more elaborate, I held myself in check for all of *nine hours*, before tugging the sterile post out, and sticking in the stone.

Have you any idea how much a five-carat diamond weighs? Imagine, for a moment, what a ball-bearing would feel like hanging out of a hole in your nose. Don't want to? Don't blame you! Each day that stone *doubled* in weight, until it felt like a car battery suspended from my nostril. Persevering for more than four months, my nose surrendered before I did. Increasingly tender, sore, and inflamed, one day it just gave up altogether. My nostril split clean in two!

The very next day I sold the limo. To hell with portents! I still have the scars to show for that little escapade.

Peace in the Valley

But it wasn't *only* the gambling that hooked me on golf. I experienced some of my most peaceful moments ever on those beautiful, breezy, manicured greens. I'd been an urban rat all my life. Alert, suspicious, and leery, I couldn't afford, even for a split second, to let my guard down. Having been a part of so much that was so ugly, my spirit felt stained, and the word *nature* wasn't even in my vocabulary.

The emotional impact of those hours spent on some of the most beautiful courses in the country was profound. I stored the images and sensations carefully, and pull them out when my spirit needs restoring.

> *I'm standing at the top of a grassy hill. It's the end of a long summer day. Dusk is closing in. Godfather is walking ahead of me, but to all intents, I'm alone. The air is still except for a rustling in the high branches of the trees and the gently persistent evening birdsong. My footfalls are cushioned by velvety grass, each blade bending for a moment under my weight then stretching back to the sky as I pass by. I walk slowly and deliberately, so as not to miss a sound. The breeze whispers, cooling and comforting, soothing and stroking. I feel it wrap around my body and soul; a cloak as real and soft as fine cashmere. In this moment, I find a well of spiritual and mental peace that has eluded me my whole life.*
> —Burrel

CHAPTER FOURTEEN

House Of Cards

1988–1990 (Age 21–23 Years)

Serena's Story

BACK IN CHI-TOWN, TYRONE, A FRIEND OF MINE, HOOKED ME UP WITH SERENA Woodson. I'd seen Serena around and had heard good things about her. Like many of the women we socialized with, she was a beautiful lady. Standing at about five feet nine inches, she was tall and slim, her bone structure fine, her nose delicate, her lips small and sculpted. Long, glossy hair framed huge eyes. In her mid-thirties, she projected the kind of seasoned *elegance* that appealed to me greatly.

Self-possessed and confident, this woman had *style*. Serena knew about packaging. She had perhaps five outfits—all designer classics—that she mixed, matched, and rotated. She'd rather spend five thousand dollars on a designer handbag than buy twenty cheaper ones with the same money.

But she was also a first-class hustler, and it was this drive that set her apart from so many of the other girls. Serena was deeply ambitious. It was written all over her face, and I *liked* it.

It transpired that her motivation was as much personal as power-driven. Her daughter, Becky, lived in Philadelphia and was being raised

137

by her grandma, Serena's mom. Now in her late teens, Becky had become estranged from her mother, and Serena, consumed by guilt, was doing everything within her power to win back her daughter's affection. Unfortunately, she decided on a strategy that seldom succeeds. She tried to buy Becky's love.

Money flowed through Serena's hands to Philly at a remarkable rate, purchasing apartments, cars, clothes, and vacations for Becky. Serena made ends meet by becoming a kind of "high-class courtesan," though one with no specific sponsor. Every month she'd spend a couple of weeks in New York hanging with some of the topflight entertainers. She'd attend every major Chicago social affair and would head South to Miami, should the need arise.

Men gave her money for no guaranteed return. Several of my friends would pass her a few thousand bucks whenever they bumped into her. On occasion, Serena might hook them up with some girls, or entertain them herself, but as I got to know her better, I realized that this woman was my kind of operator. Everything she did, she did strictly on her own terms. She joined Topflight, and soon she and I became lovers.

New Management

Golf had become something of an obsession. I *craved* the whole experience. I loved the skill and discipline; the combination of fresh air, entertainment, and exercise. I loved the game, the gamble, and the growing spiritual awareness that accompanied it all. It came to the point where business demands were just getting in the way of golf. When Serena started dropping heavy hints that she was ready for greater managerial responsibility, I was listening.

For fourteen months she'd proven herself to be competent and capable. She worked well with the other girls, was organized and focused, and had so far demonstrated that she was completely trustworthy. Our personal relationship was moving along smoothly, too. Little passion was involved, but we were getting along just fine—a blessing not to be underestimated in my volatile world.

I decided, in the summer of 1989, just after my twenty-second birthday, that I would hand over the reins of day-to-day business management to

Serena. She was duly anointed, and with light heart and lighter step, I went out to play a few holes!

New Boss, New Rules

Serena moved into pole position and immediately began to put her stamp on Topflight Services. She'd been at the helm only a few months when indications that all was not well began to bubble up. Serena was bossy and autocratic, the girls complained, and had instigated a manifesto of draconian *house rules*, such as charging fines for being late and levying an "income tax" to pay for overheads.

Worse, business was drying up. The girls just weren't getting the same number of appointments as previously, and new faces were appearing all over the place. Serena, playing favoritism, was giving her new recruits all the breaks. For many of the women, any sense of *community* evaporated.

I'd always understood these women stayed with Topflight because our setup was unique, and the benefits of operating under its umbrella, significant. We provided exclusive housing in high-priced, safe neighborhoods. The fridges were always stocked. Luxury cars, beauticians, clothes accounts, and even a vacation home were made available. The company provided unofficial medical coverage and financial advice. Calls were screened, appointments managed, security provided, and 50 percent of income retained.

All in all, it worked well, and camaraderie between the girls grew. They'd look out for each other, watch each other's backs. For some, it was a level of support not previously experienced. Of course, there were cracks; some girls would join us and stay only a short while, deciding it wasn't for them. Drug use wasn't allowed either, and anybody refusing to play by the house rules had to leave.

After our early, explosive growth, we'd settled into a period of relative stability. Many of the women had been with us for more than eighteen months, sometimes moving from city to city. Women working in Miami became friendly with the girls out of New York who would chat with the crew from L.A. Just about every nationality was represented within our network. Brits, Australians, French girls, Spaniards, Germans, Russians, Czechs, and South Africans joined dozens of beautiful Latinos, blacks, and Caucasian Americans. We were the *alternative* Miss World pageant.

We employed teachers, postal workers, models, actresses, and students. Some were extraordinarily talented, particularly true in L.A., and progressed on to outstanding career success. One or two even achieved international fame.

But the links holding it all together were fragile, too. This loose federation of women bound together by nothing more than self-interest, goodwill, and a moment in time began to unravel, bit by bit. With my head either firmly in the clouds or in a bunker, I didn't pay heed to the faint ringing of alarm bells. Defections were initially slow, just a trickle of girls heading for the door. Soon the trickle became a stream, which became a flood. In mid-1990, in just one month, forty-eight women baled from Topflight.

We would limp along for a while longer yet, but the writing was on the wall, and as it turned out, the grace period between the first rumblings of discontent and total collapse was shockingly short. I'd taken my eye off the ball, and my delayed response would be fatal for the business.

Showdown with Serena

It was clear that Serena and I were washed up on a personal level, and that things were equally precarious for us professionally. I had to clip her managerial wings and activate *damage control*.

Serena drove a green Mercedes SL. Paul Green, my Miami partner, had signed for the vehicle though I paid the note each month. With the adjustment in our relationship and the dissolution of trust, the car was forfeit. I told Paul to get rid of it. With revenues tumbling, overheads were increasingly brutal. This would be one less bill to pay. Unbeknown to me, however, Serena had been working her magic on Paul.

A buddy of his in Florida wanted the car, he told me, and was prepared to pick up the note. In reality, Serena had persuaded him to ship the car to Philadelphia. She was ready to go home to her daughter. She'd pay the monthly installments, she insisted, and was confident I need never find out.

Word trickled down that new girls were still being infiltrated into the service and Serena was redirecting clients to them. She was, in effect, siphoning off Topflight revenue to fund her own start-up business. This was tantamount to sabotage.

Upset, angry, and smarting at the betrayal, I confronted her late one night at one of our bases in downtown Chicago. The argument that followed was furious. Storming out of the apartment, she accidentally left her handbag on the sofa. With few qualms, I rifled through its contents looking for incriminating evidence. Instead, I found Western Union receipts for a car-note—a green SL 500, in fact.

The betrayal was magnified. Not only had Serena taken me to the cleaners, but Paul had, too. I knew no one was to blame but myself. I'd let my guard down badly this time, giving Serena free rein to dismantle my business right under my nose. Paul's sin may not have appeared to be so great, but he should have been watching my back. If you can't trust a man with the small things, you sure as hell can't trust him with your *life*.

I would have nothing more to do with Serena from that day on—she headed back to Philly and her lost daughter—and my relationship with Paul suffered terminal damage, though ultimately our schism couldn't *begin* to hurt him as much as he would eventually hurt himself.

Trunk Music

When I met Paul, I thought he was a really *cool* guy. In his early forties, he was mature and experienced. Not tall at five feet ten inches or so, he was beefy and dark skinned with an odd, goofy walk. He'd sort of lope along beside you, like a big, soft, floppy dog. Don't be misled though. Paul was as sharp as broken glass. Educated, by my measure anyway, he'd graduated from college and had the ability to spin words into beautiful music. Eloquent and charming, I admired him, liked him, and for a while there, thought he was the best friend a guy could have.

Paul's secret weapon was his wizardry when it came to all things financial. Known in the game as Pablo, he'd been a big name in the narcotics business until he discovered that he possessed unusual financial acumen. Paul, it transpired, was a first-rate money launderer.

Unfortunately, he wasn't quite as good at staying out of trouble. When we hooked up, he'd just finished serving an eight-year term in the penitentiary. The word was that he'd cleaned up in excess of $700 million for various dealers, including some heavyweight Colombians. None of the money was found, so the facts remained murky, but wherever you chose to put the decimal point, it fingered Paul as a *major playa*. He was certainly a useful man to know.

He liked to smoke a joint or two, sometimes snorted coke, and *loved* beautiful women. But surprisingly for a guy with such a checkered past, Paul was not too street-savvy. He was sort of *streetwise-but-straight*. He was fun, creative, and until the cracks appeared, one of my closest confidants.

We fell out over Paul's shenanigans with the girls—most notably with Serena—and over his breach of trust. The deeds to the house in Clearwater were in his name, even though the property was fully paid up, but as we weren't hanging together any longer, we planned to untangle ourselves financially.

Before we were able to do so, Paul made his bid for the big time. A few months after he and I fell out, he contacted a South Side weed dealer and convinced the guy that he was in the market for a significant shipment of *maryjane*. The dealer took Paul to a private locale and proudly showed Paul his stock of more than 240 pounds of the *good stuff*. By all accounts, they sampled a little, shot the breeze, and came to an agreement. Paul would buy as much as he needed, at six hundred bucks a pound. There was a strong likelihood that he could turn it around for almost twice that amount on the street, so when all was said and done, he was looking at a 70 percent plus profit margin. Seemed like a hell of a deal to Paul; he came away with a couple of pounds of marijuana stuffed in a duffel bag and went to work.

But Paul was no longer *plugged* into the world of narcotics. He was an outsider these days: more *white collar* than *white powder.*

I can only surmise what may have gone down. I suspect when Paul finally got the bite he desperately needed, it was from a middleman looking for weed at rock-bottom rates. Paul couldn't take it to the streets directly, and there would be little profit for him based on this deal. Something had to give. It did.

Two weeks later, in the dead of night, the warehouse was cleaned out. Hundreds of marijuana bricks gone in a puff! All two hundred plus pounds of the stuff disappeared just as surely as if it had been *smoked.*

This same warehouse location had been used for storage for years. There had never before been a breach in security. Naturally enough, suspicion fell on Paul, a recent first-time visitor. But a move like this was out of character for him—it just *wasn't* his style. Pablo was a cool, laid-back guy. His reputation was as a *behind-the-scenes* money-man, not the kind of character with the balls—or stupidity—to take on organized crime on Chicago's South Side. Cell phones buzzed; wires hummed; conferences were convened. Throughout it all, Paul protested his innocence, and for the time being, the jury was out.

The story goes that during a conversation Paul let slip some damning evidence. He knew *exactly* how much weed had gone missing, right down to the pound, a fact that had been deliberately obscured by the dealer. A few days later, Paul was missing. Two weeks after that, his body was found wrapped in black plastic, in the trunk of his Volkswagen Jetta, in a suburban parking lot. He had been shot, twice, in the back of the head. It was a cold, callous killing.

Although our friendship hadn't stood the test of time, we'd made our peace before he died. This man had been at my side for years. We'd played, partied, gambled, and smoked; we'd taken road trips and barbequed on the beach. Many a time, sitting on the front stoop of the Clearwater spread, we'd looked up at the stars and talked shit into the wee hours. No matter how often the cruel reality of wanton, untimely death hits you in the face, it never hurts any less. Paul took a piece of me with him.

The End of an Era

The property in Clearwater, Florida, was lost to me, too. Although the mortgage was paid off, the deeds were in Paul's name. All-in-all, I had more than a couple of million bucks sunk into the place. When Paul's family inherited the house and all its contents, his mother made it clear that I should pack up my personal items and move on. I was no longer welcome in Clearwater. So I did just that.

I'd taken a few too many body blows to regroup immediately. My inner voices were gaining the upper hand. I'd left the streets behind, yet I knew I carried too much of them with me. In the ghetto, I'd wielded great power, but Tony Accardo had shown me that it was just an illusion. In the wider context of the world beyond the West Side, it all fell apart.

I'd moved from the blackness of the ghetto into twilight, where my business was the provision of services to powerful, well-connected men. But the glitter of this particular game had tarnished quickly. Some of these guys may have been high-profile and politically connected, but at the end of the day, fundamentally, all of them were *weak,* and being around them weakened me.

I was still only nibbling at the edges of the life I hankered. I understood if I were to be a man of influence—a man who would leave a *positive* mark on society—it was time to step up my game, leave my bad habits behind, and fulfill my real *potential.*

I was twenty-four years old and facing yet another watershed. I had no blueprint for the next few years, but it was time to end this chapter of my life. Topflight would be terminated. I closed down operations, took a financial sucker-punch, and headed out to play a round or two.

CHAPTER FIFTEEN

Five Years On The Autobahn

1991–1995 (Age 24–28 Years)

Bad Money

EVENTS OF THE PAST COUPLE OF YEARS PROVED SOMETHING that, my whole life, I'd understood intuitively and had observed time and again. Money that comes *too easy* never sticks around, and the *wrong* kind of money can never help you do the *right* kind of things. Like trying to hold water in your hands, it'll trickle through your fingers, before evaporating into nothingness.

I've seen a hundred ghetto-millionaires who, today, don't have two pennies to rub together—my father included. Most couldn't begin to tell you how they lost their fortunes. Like a homing pigeon, bad money will *always* find its way back from where it came —and in my experience that's usually the streets.

Even fortunes earned the right way will fly out the door a thousand times faster than they flew in. Money that has never *earned* respect, sure as hell won't *give* any in return. Look at some of the young entertainers out there today, making millions in moments and spending it twice as fast. These young kids can't imagine their gravy train ever running dry, and when it does, they've no place to go. Superstar or street hustler, it makes no difference when you're broke.

I faced some harsh financial realities, but in the process, something extraordinary happened. I no longer defined myself by the magnitude of my wealth. I wore my cap to the wind. I knew that *whatever* I achieved, it would come down to my character, spirit, talent, and tenacity.

Now that felt good!

Golf Addicts

Godfather and I enjoyed each other's company. We were both emerging from rocky periods in our consistently chaotic lives and needed a little space to recover our equilibrium. The last turbulent years had hit me hard financially. I had to figure out what the next stage of my life had in store, and where my entrepreneurial spirit would drive me next. In the meantime, I was taking a break.

God also needed a change in direction. Angela had finally left him—after being at his side for more than twenty years. He was bereft without her companionship and support and had no other significant means of income. The only *skills* God could boast were gambling and golf. We decided to combine the two and take our show on the road.

We hit the fairways as though our very lives depended on it, and for a few months each year—for more than five years—we traveled the length and breadth of America on a well-worn circuit.

As usual we'd drive, not fly. Having a passion for things European—especially cars and women—I continued to favor Mercedes. These sleek, smooth, reliable workhorses were a triumph of design and performance. We ate up the miles. God would drive, and I'd doze or watch the scenery slip by, mile after mile after mile. These trips were both stimulating and soothing. Sometimes my mind would be all fired up, buzzing with plans and electricity, but mostly I emptied it of all things superfluous, and let the world shimmy by, to the rhythm of tires on tarmac.

Trundling up and down to Florida, we spent most of the winter months in Miami and Orlando, avoiding the bitter Chicago winters whenever we could. Indiana and Minneapolis were our springtime destinations, and now and again we'd make a West Coast run. Most people's *eyes* would water at the prospect of forty-plus hours of freeway stretching ahead of them, but our *mouths* did!

I understand why road trips are a great American tradition. This is one heck of a *big* country, and a beautiful one. The chase for the horizon is intoxicating: the feeling of freedom and promise and the implicit sense of *possibility*, yet-to-be-defined, but limitless. It's heady stuff. I spent the hours mulling over the past and trying to imagine what a different future could look like.

We fared pretty well on the golf course, too. I was now proficient, and God could still knock anyone for six from his knees. We'd play all day and, as dusk fell, would join other weary but satisfied players congregating in the clubhouse, or around the 19th. That's when the games *really* began. We'd offer up all kinds of tasty, little challenges: who could throw the ball nearest the tree; furthest up the hill; pitch it the greatest distance. *Dumb shit* but deceptively compelling. And highly profitable too.

We'd often end the day ahead. Heading back to our hotel, we'd gamble with each other until one of us had the other's winnings in his pocket. It took me a while to understand that I'd displaced my earlier addictions with another habit, more socially acceptable but potentially just as dangerous. I was hooked on golf just as surely as if it were a drug or dice. It left little room for anything else, least of all the multitude of business schemes gently simmering in the background.

Music

I'd dabbled in the music business for years. I've never become involved in a business that wasn't based on something I loved, and this one was no different. Promoting music seemed like a great way to indulge a passion while also making a few bucks. But I had another agenda, too. I wanted to provide a platform for my younger brother, Marcel.

A gifted drama student and musician, Marcel—a.k.a. Mr. Greenweedz—had blossomed into a talented performer. His rhyming and rapping received critical acclaim. Exuberant and charismatic, Marcel was a natural performer; his "Urban Alternative" sound was strong. But so too was the competition.

The forces that fired each of us couldn't have been more different.

Marcel was driven, but unlike me, was *not* highly motivated by money. Surrounded by piles of the stuff since he was in his cradle, he was one of the least materialistic individuals I knew. A true artist, he performed for the sake of the music and the message. For me, on the other hand, it was all about the *game* and its rewards. Our motivation may have diverged, but our goal didn't. We wanted to provide Mr. Greenweedz with a launch pad!

To create high-profile performance opportunities for Marcel, we needed to leverage the pulling power of established artists. We got serious about music promotion. Son of Burrel Entertainment was born, and another business front opened.

As I got my feet wet and became better *plugged*, my ambitions grew, too. The high point of my career as an impresario came in 1995. I was twenty-eight, and along with Tyrone decided to pull off the largest hip-hop concert Chicago had yet seen.

We chose the Amphitheater on the South Side as the stage for this coup, a venue with seating for more than five thousand. Organization for an event of this size was a massive undertaking. Public and artist response was electric, and we knew we'd have no problem filling the place. Then we hit a snag. The Amphitheater was in Gangster Disciple territory, and they wanted a slice of the action. They'd stake us half of the overhead in exchange for three thousand tickets and 50 percent of the box office.

There was *no way* that was going to happen. Markers were called in. At the time, the Disciples' boss was the legendary Larry Hoover. He was locked up in the pen, but my good friend Big John—also a GD—was able to get word to him. After a number of tense negotiations and more than a little brinkmanship, the dogs were called off.

We ended up bringing in the entire Bad Boy family. We had Craig Mac, Biggie, Puff Daddy, and Little Caesar. We also brought in Ice Cube and Bone Thugs-n-Harmony, among others. If they were hot, they were there! Mr. Greenweedz opened up, and the concert was a sizzling success.

Overall though, the music promotion business wasn't proving as profitable as I'd originally hoped. The business model I'd envisaged, somewhat naively, assumed we'd play large popular venues and share bar profits.

When it became clear that was not the way the business worked, I started booking smaller, private venues: community centers, union halls, and social clubs. I billed local talent and ran my own bar. It was a good formula and made us *twos and fews,* but on balance, it was *way* too much work for *way* too little return. Time to up the ante.

Sniffing Dust

I was still heavily involved with property development and, working with a number of crews over the preceding years, had built a solid name. By now, I had a small but impressive portfolio of modest but high quality developments under my belt.

I'd learned through trial and error just how tough this game could be. The most frustrating part of the business was the bureaucracy. Forests of paperwork were required before you could so much as stick a fork in the ground. Even with a great GC running the show, it was a slow, odious process.

Still I was committed to the game. It was gratifying to see the beginnings of a sustainable legacy, something that would endure long after I'd gone. I was proud of the work we did, and I enjoyed striding through the doors that development opened to me.

A few years earlier, I'd forged one of my best partnerships ever when I hooked up with Ed See and Stan. They'd been in the development business for years, had stellar reputations, and together we created Diamond Developments Inc. Also a May 6th Bull, Ed was honest, gritty, hardworking, ethical, and the best partner a man could hope for. His name was second to none in the business. Sixteen years on, the partnership still flourishes.

Diamond Developments didn't come by its name randomly. The name representing clarity, brilliance, and fortitude also reflected my passion for those glittering stones.

Diamonds Are Forever

Everything I know about diamonds—and that's a lot—I learned from Henry Ruzyc.

But before Henry was Young John. A diamond retailer, he had seen me around over the years and knew I was well connected. He had a proposition for me. He'd supply a range of goods—anything from basic cut stones to intricately designed jewelry—at *highly* discounted prices, I'd sell them direct, and we'd split the profits.

I sold my first few stones in less than two days, began taking orders, and within a short space of time, had sold six gold ropes, three bracelets, and five rings. I made twenty-two grand on that little lot and felt like a guy who'd won the lottery. It was time to move up the food chain.

Henry the supplier had his own store on Wabash and was the landlord of Young John's sublet. He was taciturn, caustic, and *foulmouthed*, and we hit it off right away. Verbal slap-boxing always preceded our dealings, a regular part of our business ritual, but the underlying chemistry between us was always good.

I commissioned Henry to make me a ring based on my own design of a book, pages open. The open book was a metaphor for the *transparency* of my life. The pages were composed of large diamonds nestling in a ring of smaller stones. Henry was impressed. He'd never seen a design like this, both stunning and symbolic. I had flair, he said, a natural creative talent.

After that, Henry and I collaborated on many beautiful, bespoke pieces. Fascinated by the manufacturing process and the whole craft of jewelry creation, I asked him if he'd teach *me* how to cast and mold. He said, sure, for sixty bucks an hour. Within a few months, I'd soaked up everything I could about gold, precious stones, and the business of jewelry.

In the spring of 1992, God and I had just returned from the winter golf circuit in Florida when I hooked up with a guy, who had some great contacts in the diamond business. I was invited to a high level meeting with this prospective supplier. The meeting was to take place in Monaco.

I'd always had a hankering for things European. I bought German and English cars, French champagne, and Italian suits. I admired Lady Di and the classy British actresses who showed up in old BBC productions on Chicago's cable channels. I enjoyed "Masters," the English snob in *Magnum,* and his tall tales of travel. But even though, without question a Europhile, I'd *never* had the urge to actually *visit* the damn place! Traveling across North America, coast-to-coast, was plenty global enough for me, thank you. I couldn't *imagine* that Monaco had anything to offer that I couldn't get in the good old U.S. of A.!

Still this was *business*. A man's got to do what a man's got to do. Without hesitation, I bought my ticket and, a week or so later, boarded an Air France plane to Monte Carlo via Paris. My first trip out of the States, and my mind was bursting with dreams of deals, diamonds, and dollars—not the prospect of an exotic adventure.

Monaco

Arriving mid-afternoon on a glorious sunny day, carry-on in hand, I grabbed a cab for the run to the hotel. I'll never, *ever* forget my first impressions of Monaco. It was instant infatuation!

Monaco is a small, ancient principality on the southern coast of France. It's situated on the Mediterranean, boxed in by France and the French Alps, giving you an eyeful of white-capped, mountains and blue, blue sea as you fly in. The weather is fine three hundred days a year. This day was no exception.

The entire country straddles less than single square mile. Its monarch, Prince Rainier III[20], pulled off a kind of Bugsy Siegel stroke of genius, by reinventing Monaco as a tax haven and gaming paradise. Its citizens pay no income tax. Their riches are protected by the toughest security you'll find almost anywhere on the planet. With an estimate of one officer per hundred residents, Monaco probably has more police per square foot than any other country in the world.

It's congested, overdeveloped, and glitzy. But the place still manages to ooze sophistication, class, and *old money*. Imagine an aristocratic, stunningly elegant Vegas, with a century-old heart and a glittering blue harbor packed with row after row of sparkling white yachts. I could all but taste the wealth.

A room was reserved for me at the famous Hotel de Paris located in the heart of Monte Carlo, so I went straight there from the airport. My taxi dropped me off in front of the foyer. The hotel was grand in a

---

20. In April 2005, Prince Rainier, Europe's longest reigning monarch passed away, to be succeeded by Prince Albert II. Prince Albert, the son of Prince Rainier and film star wife Grace Kelly (who died in 1982), is the thirty-second ruler of the principality.

well-bred kind of way, immaculately decorated, and dripping with exquisite furnishings and *objet d'art*. It boasted views of the palace, the Old Town, the harbor, and the casino. I freshened up, hooked up for a while with the guys I was meeting, and, then, still a little jet-lagged and a lot shell-shocked, went for a stroll.

There were wonders every which way I turned. This *had* to be happening in some alternative dimension, because a place like this couldn't possibly be of the same world I came from!

The women were gorgeous. Fine-boned, fine-complexioned, and immaculately attired. Confident, imperious, and *entitled*, they walked in a manner that said they owned the world. Judging by their jewelry and designer threads, they probably did have title to a fair slice of it. Walking along in a daze, I snatched at snippets of English conversation that rose from the swirl of other unfamiliar languages.

"Oh, no dahling. I'm talking about the *other* yacht, the one you haven't seen yet . . ."

"He lost a *fortune* last night, but you know there's just no telling him . . ."

"The Dior with the Celine? I don't think so sweetie . . ."

"I told him *I* need the helicopter tomorrow . . ."

I was feeling lightheaded and needed a sugar-fix. After paying the equivalent of six bucks for a Snickers bar that at home cost only seventy-five cents or so, I chewed thoughtfully, while calculating how much profit I could make by flogging a few cases on the street corner for three bucks a bar. Hmm. Time to hit the casino.

Tuxedo Junction

The Monte Carlo Casino has a legendary reputation, and I dressed in a manner suitable for a visit to what is possibly the world's most *elegant* gambling hall. I'd packed my Armani tuxedo and bundles of cash. Armed with both, I sauntered into the casino like one of my Rat Pack heroes. Working my way through the marble-paved, onyx-columned lobby and the outer gaming rooms, I entered the salons.

Richly decorated with stained glass, sculptures, and artwork, the rooms were stunning. I knew I was walking through *history*. Acclimatizing quickly, I looked around. This was nothing like Vegas! The gentle tug of conversation lapped through the room, restrained chatter blending with the *click, clack, click* of chips and dice and roulette wheels. It was early in the evening, and I meandered around the tables watching, listening, and steeping myself in the ambience.

As time went on, the serious players began arriving, the piles of chips growing taller with the increase in wealth-quotient. Elegant men and women wafted around, balancing stacks of five-thousand-dollar chips some a foot high, in wooden trays on their arms. I wandered, watched, and *marinated* until I began to feel a little naked without gambling currency. I went to buy my own chips in the game, twenty of them to be precise.

Swaggering out of the hotel that night, with twenty grand stashed in my jacket, I'd felt like *Mr. Big Shot*. But now, having transformed that bundle into a little puddle of cheap chips clutched in one hand, I felt more like a farm boy on his first visit to the big city.

I regrouped quickly, though, and was soon weaving my way around the tables like a pro. It was while I was standing at a roulette table watching the game, that a beautiful, elfin-faced woman slipped into the space next to me. Dark-haired and delicate, she was all *silk* and *scent*.

She didn't look directly at me: "You're not playing tonight?" Her accent was French and husky, sending a pleasant little shiver shimmying down my spine.

I did my best James Bond: "No, ma'am. Just taking my time and getting a feel for the tables." Shaken not stirred.

"Well, I have a good feeling about number *eighty-one*," she motioned toward the wheel. "Here, let me . . ."

With that, she extended a finely bejeweled hand and leaned across to take a few chips from my stack.

I reacted like any self-respecting West Side boy caught in a stickup. I *snatched* those chips out of her reach faster than the *Ricochet Rabbit*!

"*Are you kidding, lady*?" My voice had gone up an octave or two. "Get your *own* damn chips!"

She shook her head in wonder. "Its just a *measly* few thousand dollars," she snapped. "What are you so worried about?"

The damage was done, and my exotic angel departed in the kind of elegant, perfumed huff that only the French so effortlessly achieve. I congratulated myself on my escape and continued my vigil.

153

The next night I was back, with the same twenty chips. The evening wore on, and the casino was humming with activity when I glimpsed her. She was sitting across the room at a crowded blackjack table, and was almost eclipsed by the stacks of five-thousand-dollar chips lined up in front of her, like a small regiment. I'd been chatting with another casino patron, a local, and nudged him with a nod in her direction: "Now, *she's* a piece of work. Wonder which sucker she scammed tonight."

He looked at me incredulously. "Are you referring to Lady Veronique? *No, no, no.* She is rich. Very, *very* rich! Every single night she is here. In fact . . ." he led me by the arm to a window and gestured toward a magnificent, floodlit villa positioned on what had to be one of the most prime pieces of real estate in Monte Carlo. "She lives just over there."

He looked at me pityingly and then moved away quickly. Perhaps he thought stupidity was contagious. I'll always wonder what might have been with Lady Veronique, if I'd only bet on *eighty-one.*

As for the rest of my short visit to Wonderland, well, it just flew by. I had a couple of good business meetings, though ultimately little came of them, and headed for home, you guessed it, with a head full of deals, diamonds, and dollars.

Monaco did nothing but fire up my appetite for a different kind of life. I resumed my routine, playing golf, selling jewelry, and pursuing development projects, but it was startlingly apparent that something had to change—if I was ever going to be the kind of guy with a yacht tied up in the harbor and a Lady Veronique on his arm.

> *Burrel was always raising the bar, shaking himself up, and reinventing himself. He was comfortable playing in any arena. He showed us all we could bridge the divide between race and class.*
>
> —Big C

Wenny: The Final Act

Wenny never did plan on leaving the streets, but in the end any say he may have had in the matter was taken away from him. It was ironic that after years of doing people down, Wenny was murdered for something he *didn't do*.

It was 1994. Wiz had been hanging with a gang chief I'll call M. Wenny was a Mafia Vice Lord by this time, as was M. Quite a few Cicero Insane gang-bangers had shifted allegiance a couple of years earlier, and the Mafia had grown to be a powerful crew in the West Side.

This particular evening M and Wiz were attending another gang-banger's birthday bash, a guy known as Twin. Twin was a member of the Conservatives. It wasn't unusual for different factions, in a specific geography, to rub shoulders. This mix of gangs, alcohol, and guns could be incendiary, but though affiliated with different crews, many guys hailed from the same 'hoods. They'd grown up together, families knew families and had ties going back years, and as long as no one was looking for trouble, they could usually muddle through an evening without adding to the body count.

A week or so after the party, M ran across Twin and a friend of his, Kurt, selling merchandise on Mafia territory. M warned them off. They made all the right noises, and themselves scarce. Unconvinced, M hung around, and, sure enough, the next day, they were right back in the same spot.

As soon as he saw he'd been *double-clutched*, M called a move. He ordered one of his "little guys," Ricky, to hit both Kurt and Twin. These young cats were the *worst*. They wanted to be as bad as the *baddest* guy ahead of them, and a ten-year-old could be more callous and vicious than a seasoned fighter. Ricky went after Kurt and Twin like a missile.

Both boys ran. Their car was parked close by and they jumped into it, but before they could even get the key in the ignition, Ricky came alongside and shot Twin dead, at point blank range. Kurt jumped out, scrambling for his life. He didn't stand a chance. He took a bullet to the head and died instantly.

Unbeknown to M or Ricky, there was a passenger in the backseat of the car. A young local girl had witnessed the whole thing go down, before curling into a ball, scrunching up her eyes, and *praying* that no one spotted her. Her prayers were answered. M and Ricky, slapping themselves on the backs for a job well done, moved right along.

All hell broke loose when Twin's bother heard what had gone down.

He got together with the Conservative *influential,* and fingers were pointed. M was easily identified as the perpetrator, and as he and Wenny had partied together just the week before, Wiz was fingered, too, tainted by association.

The tension between the Conservatives and the Mafia reached boiling point. After intense consultations within the Conservative leadership clique, all-out war was declared against the Mafia.

Amid all this noise, Wenny frantically tried to extricate himself from the whole goddamn mess. He went to meet Twin's mom and family and explained that he'd had nothing to do with the executions; that he'd known Twin and Kurt for years and would never have done this to them. He'd been entirely unaware of M's intent, he claimed, and would have stopped him had he known what was on his mind. Finally, he promised he would *check* M, and personally administer an appropriate punishment.

They gave the appearance of listening, but Wiz's protestations of innocence fell on deaf ears. Twin's family, and by extension the Conservatives, remained convinced that Wenny and M had been in cahoots all along. For once in his life, Wiz's silver tongue failed him. Problem was, he wasn't quite smart enough to know it yet.

Wenny was caught in one of those Catch-22s. To reinforce his claims of innocence, he had to show his face in Twin's neighborhood: the *I grew up wi'j'all, so I can hang here* kinda thing. But to do so was more than a little risky. In the all-out gang war now raging, no one was exempt, least of all Wiz.

One evening, not long after the shooting, Wenny headed down to Conservative turf to gamble. He'd just bought a new Volvo, and one of the neighborhood guys came into the pool hall whistling with admiration: "Tha's yo' Volvo, Wiz? Take this nigga for *a ride,* man."

Wiz was happy to oblige. "Sure, man. She's like silk," he boasted. "You won't find another lady as *smooth* and *hot* as this bitch."

"Cool, man. C'mon then. Take me outside."

The Volvo was parked in front of the pool hall, a spanking new, sparkling white 760. After walking around the car a few times and running his hands along its smooth lines, the guy tells Wenny to pass him the keys so he can get a feel for her. Wenny tosses him the keys and climbs in the passenger side.

He probably saw the young kid in the wing mirror before he heard the shots. We'll never know for certain, but Wiz wasn't the kind of guy who missed much, so my money says that he saw it all unfold. I imagine his gaze colliding for a split second with that of his would-be assassin and, in that bitter moment, seeing the stark, bleak reality of his own death—and life. He took two shots to the head, blood and brains splattering the dashboard of his beautiful new car. He died instantly. Wenny was thirty years old.

My good friend Keke and I paid for his funeral. I grieved for Wenny, but I guess that's how it goes down. I've seen too much that appears to be so inherently unfair that sometimes it's hard to believe life isn't just a roll of the dice.

There's the good guy who loses his woman to a cheating, violent asshole. Or the guy who gets fifteen for burglary, while the cold-blooded murderer wriggles through the net. I've seen guys killed because they left the house five minutes early, or five minutes late, or because someone with a gun was in a bad mood that night. I've seen guys shot in cases of mistaken identity, boys who are dead or crippled because they were in the wrong place at the wrong time and caught a ricochet. Then again, I've seen men—like God—survive with thirteen bullets pumped *point blank* into their bodies.

I believe in fate, but at the same time, my heart doesn't accept its randomness. Our relationship with the Universe is not passive. Every ounce of wit, energy, and intelligence we have has to be applied to improve the hand we've been dealt, and without fail, we must always— *always*— play fair.

In all the years I knew him, Wenny *never* played fair. His hand needn't have been a losing one, but he ensured it was. In the end, there was certain tragic symmetry between the way he lived and the manner in which he died.

CHAPTER SIXTEEN

Venture Capitalist Adventures

1996–1999 (Age 29–32 Years)

Back to the Farm

In the summer of 1995, Burrel Senior had packed his bags and headed back to the small holding in Mississippi. There was nothing in Chicago to keep him. Everything he'd made from the streets had gone back to the streets, leaving only the wreckage of his body, mind, and spirit in its wake. Jonnie had called him one night and threatened to disinherit him. The house and the land were the last cards in Burrel Senior's deck. Wisely, he went on home.

My dad left reluctantly, but it was still a choice made more or less on his own terms. Leaving the streets requires more than a change of address, though; it requires a whole new state of mind. No matter where you go the streets will be *right* behind. Unless you can look them in the eye and say *no,* they'll follow you forever. My Dad was finally saying no.

Some guys, like my dad, cut off all links except family. I can understand why. The streets, you see, have this way of pulling you back. Give them a *minute*, and they'll take a *lifetime*.

But the West Side was—and is—a part of me. I still visited regularly, saddened by its drastic decline. These blocks had always been raw, rough, and risky, but whatever vigor had radiated from the neighborhood was extinguished, displaced by depression and despondency. You could *smell* hopelessness which rose like steam from the pavements. Faces were familiar, but the hard, hungry eyes of strangers looked back at me. These streets were no longer my reality.

Seasoned

On the threshold of my third decade, I viewed the landscape with wonder. Where was that brash teenager who'd set off to tackle the world, pockets full of cash and a head full of dreams? But though older, wiser, and more circumspect, my spirit was stronger than ever. I was, at heart, *still* that irrepressible, excited kid, racing around the next bend in the road.

And I was *rich* with experience. I'd chased dreams, pursued passions, and honed skills that would be with me forever. Businesses flourished and faltered, the failures harsh, the successes spectacular. Along the way, great friendships were forged; I fell in and out of love and fathered sons as well as two wonderful daughters.

I'd tasted hardship, too. Wrestling with addiction and demons, I'd lost friends and fortunes, felt the sting of betrayal, and had my heart broken more than once. And I'd seen *far too much* death. Bloodied maybe, but certainly not bowed, I was seasoned. When I checked my cards that day in May 1997, my hand was definitely a *winner*. Given the opportunity, I knew I'd play those same cards over again.

To kick off my fourth decade in style, my thirtieth birthday was to be a lavish, boisterous affair. Big C and I combined resources and threw a huge party. We were both May 6th Bulls. Big C had been a heavyweight player back in the eighties, and by rights, we shouldn't have been close— he was a Soul and I was a Vice Lord. Under the skin, though, we felt as though we were *brothers-from-another-mother* and, against all odds, built an enduring friendship.

A couple of hundred people came to our party, representing all backgrounds, lifestyles, denominations, and occupations. It was as eclectic a crowd as you could ever hope to see, and I looked around and understood these faces were a reflection of the fullness of my life and experiences. Friends, family, and partners, past and present, mingled with developers, financiers, and escorts, who mingled with pimps, sportsmen, businessmen, and gang-bangers.

Champagne flowed, the band played, and like those days in my basement apartment, a lifetime ago, we *stepped* the night away.

Personal maturation heralded changes in my business outlook, too. These days I wanted to invest in more *solid* ventures. I yearned for real bricks and mortar, places that actually sold *stuff* and couldn't evaporate overnight. I'd always been my own venture capitalist and funded my own businesses, but now I was ready to share the heavy-lifting. Time to play the partnership game.

Carried Away with Cars

In 1997, in collaboration with a buddy named Dusco, I became partner in a car dealership. Dusco owned a small service station in the west suburbs and, like me, was passionate about cars. Our dazzling love affair with high-end rides may have blinded us both to some of the harsher realities of an ugly, dog-eat-dog business.

After investing, jointly, in a handful of luxury cars, we successfully auctioned them off, with little effort, for a tidy profit. I have to admit we both got a little overexcited; our ambitions went on steroids!

We bought a tract of land and, over the next two years, developed it into a showcase for luxury cars. We poured millions into the venture; our state-of-the-art showroom was firmly wedged between two enormous dealerships in a prime location. Flanked by Toyota and Lexus, we outshone both, on the surface at least.

Supply wasn't a problem. "Gently-used" Rolls, Bentleys, BMWs, and Mercedes could be sourced with ease, and there were no shortage of interested customers either. They were all but lining up at the door.

No, our problems were in the *back office*. The big financial institutions weren't prepared to get into bed with us. As a consequence, we couldn't offer our clients the kind of credit and financing options they required. Deals were falling through right, left, and center. The big boys were basically telling us to stop trying to *piss in the tall weeds* and go home.

Left with a vast car lot, peppered with no more than thirty cars, when it could easily have swallowed three hundred without chewing, we faced shocking overhead and image problems. The trickle of cash flow became the gurgle of "cash drain." It was only a matter of time before we'd have to pull the plug.

Real Bricks and Mortar

Diamond Developments, in the meanwhile, continued to prosper. Our reputation was soaring. Construction of a couple of sizeable, commercial complexes was completed to high standards, and we were getting some great press. With a portfolio spanning condominiums, townhomes, shopping malls, and community centers, Diamond was the jewel in the crown.

I extended my personal interests, buying into a couple of long-term projects, such as a chain of gas stations, but having learned some of the harder facts about the world of financing, I made sure I took a slice of the "behind-the-scenes" action, too. There was as much money to be made in the mortgage and insurance game as there was in laying the actual bricks.

Ambitious Designs

My love affair with design had taken root way back in '86 with the lavish furnishing of my dream home in Old Oak Brook. I discovered then, that the markup on high-end furniture could exceed 200 percent and immediately began dreaming about opening my own furniture store. In 1999, the dream became reality.

In partnership with Michelle, a gifted designer, I uncovered the perfect location: 4000 square feet of light, bright showroom space fronting one of the busiest intersections in Chicago's River North area. Then in order to secure the hard-to-get product lines we needed, I headed to North Carolina and waded into one of the largest furniture shows in the world: the International Home Furnishings Market in High Point.

This vast, glittering convention reminded me a little of Monaco. (The venue itself certainly felt about the same size as that tiny country, as I traversed back and forth on complaining feet, but there was more to it than that. The place was like a glittering gathering of the jet set.) Exhibitors—many of them European—hosted cocktail parties or coffee lounges, where glamorous people fluttered like flocks of colorful birds. Unlike Monoco, instead of watching them gamble, here you watched them buy exquisite pieces of *room art*. There's no question that a beautiful piece of furniture is like a fine collectible—boasting forms as elegant as sculpture and textures as rich as a haute couture evening gown. When all was said and done, I loved these trips and was highly successful in sourcing some magnificent collections.

The doors of Unique Designs opened in late 1999, and in 2000, the NASDAQ bubble burst with the force of a nuclear explosion and the last of my paper fortune vaporized just as certainly as if it had taken a direct hit. I lost my shirt, pants, jacket, and pension plan all in a few short moments. Financially, I was right back to square one.

Call it what you will—hustling, deal making, or just plain business—at the end of the day, like most entrepreneurs, I *lived* for the thrill of the chase, the game around the game, and the ultimate prize of closing the sale. But something had changed. I still loved the hustle and tumble, but it was clear that my center of gravity had shifted. My mind was still scheming, planning, and working the numbers, but my heart was tugging me in a different direction. I'd arrived at a critical junction on a long personal and emotional voyage. I wanted—no, needed—to begin *giving back*.

CHAPTER SEVENTEEN

Bittersweet Years

2001–2004 (Age 34–37 Years)

Fishing for Minds

"LET ME INTRODUCE MYSELF. I'M BURREL LEE WILKS III. The reason I'm here today is to help you change *your* lives. Because, you see, *I see your future* more clearly than you do."

The kids in the front row studiously avoid eye contact, except a youth, stocky and slouched, who watches me defiantly, and a bright-eyed, light-skinned girl studying my face like it's a map.

"You wanna know how that can be? How suddenly I'm a fortune-teller?"

A murmur rustles through the room.

"I'll *tell* you how. Because *I've been* down that road y'all goin down . . . and I was the best. *I mean THE BEST!*"

I scan the audience, reading their faces. They're paying attention now.

"But I'm here to tell you: *don't* take that same road I did. Because I guarantee—*guarantee*—you ain't goin' to be as lucky as I was."

I walk slowly across the front of the stage, making eye contact with the kids in front. Everyone's sitting up.

"You think what y'all doin' is new? You think you're the first to give your teachers a hard time when they try to shape your mind, and then hit the streets as soon as school is out, tryin' to be P. Diddy tonight?"

Even the sloucher has uncrossed his arms and is watching me intently.

"No, it'd be *plain stupid* to think that. And *none* of you are *stupid*. In fact, I'm here to tell you you're already *way smarter* than any of those gang-bangers out there." I indicate the windows. "Do you know why you're smarter?"

A couple of kids are itching to answer, hands twitch but don't quite make it.

"Because you're here *improving* your minds, *growing* your brains, and *building* your future! But that gang-banger out there, he's just *one step* away from the penitentiary or his own *personal* hole in the ground."

Ready-Set-Work

Ready-Set-Work, a nonprofit foundation, was created as a response to the terrible pressures so many inner-city kids face every day. Neither qualified academically, nor prepared mentally to enter the workforce, they were falling through the social cracks like lemmings.

These were tough times. The character of the 'hoods had changed. OG and newcomer alike, if you didn't have a place in the new order, or wanted to disengage, your options were limited. Once the attraction of the streets had worn thin, few youngsters had a Plan B. The odds of these kids getting a fair shot at a different kind of life were negligible. The saddest part of it all is that so many of them would give it a go—if they only knew how. There were, and are, a great many lost, confused kids out there.

These days my phone was hotter than *cayenne pepper* with guys pouring out their troubles in return for advice, guidance, and motivation. The need was clear, and when Ready-Set-Work approached me, it was a natural progression to get on stage and take my message to the schools, and to the kids. Over the next couple of years, we talked to hundreds of youngsters, so many of whom were wrestling with the kind of choices that would determine whether they survived, thrived, or even *died*.

I had a hundred tales, anecdotes, metaphors, and real-life experiences in my hard-hitting repertoire, and I used them to explain the importance of gaining an education, staying out of gangs, and staying off drugs. I'd try to help these kids understand the long-term value of having a square job versus the momentary satisfaction of a street deal. Sure, they might only earn seven bucks an hour flipping burgers at McDonalds, but compare that to the sixteen bucks a month they *may* pull down, mopping floors in the pen. And that's if they made it there *alive*.[21]

Breaking the ice was easy enough. I'd introduce myself, briefly run through my *street résumé* and ask them who were the players in their 'hood. I'd stayed close enough to the ghetto to know what was going down, and could usually tell them more about their crew, and its history, than they knew themselves.

What I didn't do was judge.

"I can't tell you to *stop* doin' what *you been* doin'," I told them as I walked among the rows of chairs, looking into their faces one-by-one.

"Why?"

"I'll tell you why. I can't tell you to *stop* because I din't tell you to *start*. But I *sure as hell* can tell you what's goin' down if you keep on doin' what you doin'."

If they didn't take hold of their lives now, I told them, they could die or *get behind the eight ball*, that is, end up in the pen. There was only one person who could change things, I explained. Themselves. The motivation and strength had to come from inside, but they'd have to reach *deep* because this was *not* easy stuff.

We talked a lot about choices—smart choices and dumb ones. I watched those kids, looked into their eyes, and read their body language. I knew I touched them. And I knew that this was what I wanted to do with my life. I wanted to touch *all* those kids.

---

21. Several sources for social, economic, mortality, education, and crime statistics have previously been cited in this book, but in my opinion, one of the most provocative and cohesive presentations of facts and figures relating to the economic and social development of the African-American population in the USA is to be found woven into the pages of Michael Eric Dyson's book: *Is Bill Cosby Right? Or Has the Black Middle Class Lost Its Mind?* (Basic Civitas Books, 2005).

> "Too many kids get sucked into the dark side because they don't know how to say no. They don't think they have options. Most kids are good kids—they just get lost. Burrel's got the map that shows the way home."
> —Bobby Simmons

Freeway Freefall

I met my wife on the freeway.

I was exiting Route 94, veering onto Ohio, the sharply curved slip road that would take me into downtown Chicago, and home. It was about 7:30 in the evening, warm with the promise of summer just around the corner. I was tired and preoccupied, my brain as usual, chockablock.

This little silver bullet of a car came from behind and shot past on the inside lane, unceremoniously jerking me back to the present. Side by side, we each hugged the curve too tightly, then in a blur, she was gone. It took a split second. In that moment, I caught a glimpse of the woman who would become my wife.

How did I get her to stop? Well, I put my foot down and, at the first set of traffic lights we came to, pulled up parallel, wound down my window, and attempted to strike up a conversation. At first, she resisted, pointedly ignoring me and keeping her eyes firmly fixed ahead. I repeated the process at the next three sets of lights. There was no shaking me. Maybe it was my perseverance or perhaps it was my smile but whatever the reason, that little silver car pulled into the curbside behind me, as we entered the downtown area.

On the surface, we were polar opposites. She was a serious and buttoned-down Brit, vice president in a large corporation; I was a passionate, risk-taking West Side boy. She had traveled to more than forty countries, lived on three continents, and been around the globe three times that year. I hadn't. She had trekked through mangrove swamps in Southern Burma, canoed on the Amazon, and watched the arrival of the new millennium from the back of a horse in the desert in Jordan. I'd brought in the new millennium too in the desert—drinking Cristal in Vegas.

I talked her into drinks and dinner that night, and within a week, I knew this woman would be a permanent fixture in my life. I had my first good night's sleep in years.

We married two years later.

> " *I think about it often. Our lives intersected for, what, three or four seconds? Don't tell me that wasn't fate. What if I hadn't driven as fast, or he'd driven faster, or if either of us had set off a minute earlier, or later. I'll never really understand what made me stop, but there is without a doubt something rare, and compelling, about this man.* "
>
> —Janet Fitzpatrick-Wilks

Flush with Faith

Know what a winning poker hand looks like? For years, I had everything I needed for my winning hand, except a queen. Now I'd found her, and my royal flush was complete. In August 2002, I had a full hand of hearts tattooed on my arm, so I could appreciate it every day.

I chose hearts over spades, because my whole life I'd played every card with passion. As an expression of this commitment, I added an evergreen framework around my royal flush, symbolic of the fact that I would go to my grave *playing with heart.*

Like most people, my faith is made up of a mosaic of beliefs, not a single formula. I'm deeply spiritual but not religious. I meditate, often lost within myself or in the clouds and stars, for hours on end. My faith sustains me. I feel privileged and blessed to be alive and healthy. There is a *reason* I'm still here, and I intend to make the most of the energy, insight, and knowledge I have been blessed with, to positively influence the lives of others.

I sense patterns in the universe, a fatalistic faith that has helped me cope with the vicissitudes of life. Every shred of this faith was called on, the day I learned my son had been murdered.

Marshawn

I first became a father at the age of fifteen.

I'd met Marshawn's mother, Pam Givens, the previous summer when I was just fourteen. We got on well, had fun together. When Marshawn was conceived, I was happy with the idea of bringing a son into the world. At the time, though, I was all about business, had little place for fatherhood in my short-term plans, and was nowhere near ready for this kind of responsibility.

A brash, ferociously ambitious young gang chief, I was juggling hundreds of dynamics daily, hustling my heart out, consolidating my power base, fortifying my business, and wrestling with demons and drugs. I didn't have a lot of room left for anything else. I didn't *push* to become involved in my son's upbringing, and although he was on my mind often, we had little contact across the years, something I regret very much.

In 2001, Marshawn reappeared in my life unexpectedly. He was nineteen, I was thirty-five, and the timing couldn't have been better. It was a second chance for both of us. I was ready to have my son home.

An open-faced, bright boy, Marshawn was the image of me physically. Though a little shorter, he had the same solid build, clear dark eyes, and warm chestnut complexion. Facially, from his hairline and high cheekbones to his wide white smile, he could have been my clone. To see him sitting on the sofa was uncanny. Here was a reflection of myself as a much younger man, but with the clear stamp of a unique and individual personality.

Our mutual resemblance certainly didn't extend far beyond the physical. While Marshawn had inherited my love of the hustle and my thickheadedness, he had *not* inherited my drive, focus, savvy, and leadership skills: skills necessary to survive in the ghetto. He was a small-time hustler, dabbling in a few lightweight scams and just *getting by* playing a bit of pool, dealing some cards, and selling a little weed.

Marshawn's reentry into my life was a blessing, a God-sent chance to hurdle over too many lost years and get to know my son. Both of us wanted to spend more time together, so in early 2002 Marshawn moved his belongings into my penthouse.

Over the subsequent summer months, we'd hang, drive, smoke, and talk. I started to get to know this quiet, circumspect young man, but had the sense that he was only allowing me to scratch the surface. It was proving hard to rebuild bridges that had long since been burned.

Marshawn was already set on his course in life. He listened but didn't hear my counseling.

Still, that was okay. I was patient. We had time.

No More Sunrises

Marshawn died one night in October 2002.

I'd been away from home that night and, unusually, had let my cell phone run out of juice. It hadn't worried me. I wasn't expecting any urgent calls.

Arriving home the following morning just after ten a.m., I walked through the kitchen and saw the fifty dollars I'd left out for Marshawn, the day before, was still sitting on the countertop. He'd told me he needed a few bucks for a party he was going to. He must have changed his plans, I thought.

With the cell phone recharged, I picked up the backlog of voice-mail messages. My cousin had called me a number of times, the frustration and tension in his voice transparent, as he failed, again and again, to reach me. With obvious reluctance, he'd finally left a detailed message, informing me that my son had been shot dead.

The story was tawdry and tragic. Marshawn had been hanging out with a couple of buddies, one a childhood friend. They'd been out and about looking for action and were sitting in his buddy's car, having a smoke when a squabble broke out over a girl. In moments, Marshawn was dead. That's all it was: a *dumb-assed, stupid, ignorant* battle of words and testosterone that exploded into a *killing*.

I'd witnessed senseless, meaningless violence and pointless death time and again, but *nothing* had prepared me for the shock of my son's murder—and the pain of his loss. The despair was indescribable, a chaotic kaleidoscope of emotion that left me with a hole in my heart and a new set of demons to battle.

Thoughts circled relentlessly throughout many a long, dismal predawn hour. What if I'd played a fuller role in his life, would things have turned out differently? What if I'd pushed him harder to get a job? What if I'd found a job *for* him and forced him to take it? Maybe I should have grounded him that night? On and on, my mind circled: "what if, what if." I lay awake night after night posing questions that could never be answered.

171

At fifteen years old, what kind of a role model would I have been for my son? As I struggled down my own path learning my own tough lessons through trial and error, would I have set my son on the *right* road? Or like my father, would I have brought my son, Marshawn, along to share my own turbulent and dangerous ride?

Miracles happen when you least expect them. In the midst of the darkness, I discovered I was to become a grandfather.

Grandfather

I knew Marshawn had been dating a girl from Rockford, but he and I hadn't mended our broken fences well enough to fully confide in each other. Now we never would. Marshawn certainly hadn't shared with me that his girlfriend was pregnant, and that he was to become a father sometime in early 2003. This incredible news only became apparent, when I came face to face with May at my son's funeral.

May and I were introduced. Young and pale with sadness, she appeared shy but strong, too. We talked for a while, and I promised her that I would be there for my grandchild.

The funeral and memorial services were attended by crowds of people wishing to pay their respects to Marshawn, and to his family. Family, friends, and acquaintances turned up in droves, milling, huddling, and chatting somberly about the frightening fragility of life.

God was traveling with me that day, in case I lost it, and needed to hand over the wheel to someone. I was comfortable driving, for the moment. I needed to keep busy, keep moving. That's how God came to be in the passenger seat as the police pulled us over. They ordered us out of the car, and searched the vehicle, uncovering only my son's obituary.

I scanned the scene, registering the angry faces of onlookers, *outraged* that cops would stop and search a grieving father as he left his son's graveside. They'd been looking for a gun, certain that I was an OG with vengeance on his mind.

Nothing could have been further from the truth. There was no gun, no bitterness, and no thoughts of retribution, just the sad, hollow knowledge that I'd lost my son and that we were all trapped inside one kind of a cell or another. Mine was my past.

Chicago is my home. This city has given me everything I have, and taken back whatever it pleased. These streets are my past, but they are *not* my prison. I knew—with startling clarity—that it was finally time to cut myself loose from the emotional shackles that had bound me for too long. It was time to close one book, and move my life boldly forward, in order to write the first chapter of the next volume.

The rattle of handcuffs dropping from my wrists was joined by the clatter of the chains falling from my mind.

Bridging The Divide

TODAY MY LIFE IS DIVIDED BETWEEN THE WEST COAST, CHICAGO, AND ALL POINTS IN BETWEEN. I am a Life Coach with a flourishing practice, and a successful businessman with a vision. I plan to do everything in my power to *bridge the divide* between the kids who've been left behind and the world of *possibility*.

I'm one of the lucky ones, but stories like mine—stories of *transformation* and *celebration*—are far too few. At the end of the day, this story is not really about me, but about the kids who are left behind, the ones who fall through the cracks.

The streets are seductive and deadly. They promise money, power, and instant gratification. They create the illusion of vitality but, in reality, offer only dead-ends and hopelessness. Their pull is strong. Most kids believe they go to them on their own terms. Trust me, they're deluding themselves. The ghetto's a *quagmire*. It sucks you in, pulls you under, and spits you out when it's done. The choice is not yours.

Heroic battles are enacted every single day, as kids struggle to do the right thing. They want to break away all right, but hemmed in by too many temptations and too few alternatives, they just *don't know how*. Without effective role models, *generations* of youngsters are lost to us.

In a sense, I'm a voice for all the pent-up, pinned-down talent and ambition that lives in the heads and hearts of so many youngsters who've little hope of escaping, with no paper *qualification* or *certification.*

I want to show them that anything is possible, that they can't allow their birthright to define them or conditioning to constrain them. I want to show them that they are building their own jails, from the inside out, but though they've put themselves in lockup, they already have the combination to get out. I want to help them step out into the sunlight.

My dream is to put the right kind of tools and resources into their hands, tools that will help them say "no" to the streets and "yes" to an alternative path. I plan on using all my wits, insight, energy, and connections to do so.

When I close my eyes, I can see myself all those years ago, the *unspoiled* parts of me shining through: a bright-faced, scrappy, lippy little kid, drinking up his dad's words, tangling himself in all kinds of mischief, strutting his stuff on street corners, scrapping and skating, bragging and boasting, jumping off the back of moving trucks, and driving along the lakeshore on balmy summer nights.

I want to hold out my hand to that boy, and all the boys like him. And I want to celebrate the miracle that he is here today, with his body, heart, and soul intact, living proof of the *power of transformation.*

Bibliography

With much appreciation for the work of these authors:

Binder, John. *The Chicago Outfit*. Arcadia Publishing, 2004.

Bromfield, Ann, Don Juan and Katheryn L. Patterson. *From Pimp Stick to Pulpit—It's Magic: The Life Story of Don "Magic" Juan*. Vantage Press, 1994.

Dawley, David. *A Nation of Lords: The Autobiography of the Vice Lords*. Waveland Press Inc., 1992.

Dyson, Michael Eric. *Is Bill Cosby Right? Or Has the Black Middle Class Lost Its Mind?* Basic Civitas Books, 2005.

Enright, Laura L. *Chicago's Most Wanted: The Top 10 Book of Murderous Mobsters, Midway Monsters and Windy City Oddities*. Potomac Books Inc., 2005.

Kotlowitz, Alex. *There Are No Children Here: The Story of Two Boys Growing Up in the Other America*. Anchor Books, 1991.

Levitt, Steven D. and Stephen J. Dubner. *Freakonomics: A Rogue Economist Explores the Hidden Side of Everything*. William Morrow, 2005.

McWhorter, John. *Losing the Race: Self-Sabotage in Black America*. The Free Press, 2000; Perennial, 2001.

Perkins, Useni Eugene. *Explosion of Chicago's Black Street Gangs: 1900 to Present*. Third World Press, 1987.

Russo, Gus. *The Outfit: The Role of Chicago's Underworld in the Shaping of Modern America*. Bloomsbury, 2003.

I would also like to thank the designers, architects, and custodians of the dozens of Web sites dedicated to aspects of urban culture, and in particular Chicago's urban landscape, communities, and history. These sites provided a wealth of information, context, and color. Thank you for providing such a valuable service, often voluntarily.

Index